COLORS IN
CAMBRIDGE
GLASS

By

National Cambridge Collectors, Inc.

COLLECTOR BOOKS

A Division of Schroeder Publishing Co., Inc.

Searching For A Publisher?

We are always looking for knowledgeable people considered to be experts within their fields. If you feel that there is a real need for a book on your collectible subject and have a large comprehensive collection, contact Collector Books.

COLLECTOR BOOKS
P.O. Box 3009
Paducah, Kentucky 42002-3009
or
National Cambridge Collectors, Inc.
P.O. Box 416
Cambridge, Ohio 43725

Printed by IMAGE GRAPHICS, INC., Paducah, Kentucky

ACKNOWLEDGEMENTS

No book of this scope can be accomplished by one individual. This study aid for Cambridge colors represents the combined efforts of a large group of dedicated, hard working and generous members and friends of National Cambridge Collectors, Inc. We gratefully acknowledge the assistance and cooperation of the following contributors:

Mary and Jack Adams
Evelyn and Tony Allen
Jo and Gerald Barstow
Barbara Beye
Kathy Bierman
Clara and Ray Brown
Jean and Paul Carter
Carol, Lee and Martin Coppo
Betty and Jim Cusick
Betty and Bob Dasen
Karen and Tom Germani
Gail Grabow
Phyllis and Frank Hayes
Sally and Bob Hayler
Mary and Wilbur Henderson
Virginia and Dick Houston
Janice and Larry Hughes
Norma, Willard and David Kolb
Ruby and Gerald Landman
Florence and Joseph Lipper
Dorothea and Arnold Lynd
Joy McFadden
Debbie and David Nielsen
Naomi Opphile

Sue and Dave Rankin
Jane and Don Rogers
Henrietta Ruhl
Phyllis, Bill, Ed and Mark Smith
Deborah and Dennis Snyder
Patricia and Charles Stocker
Elaine and Dick Storck
Meg and Bill Turner
Bonnie Van Sickle
Jo Ann and Russel Vogelsong
Carlene and Paul Voytko
Norma and Donald Warden
Mary, Lyle and Lynn Welker
Donna Williams
Vicki and Frank Wollenhaupt
Others who wish to remain anonymous
National Cambridge Collectors study groups:
    The California Cambridge Collectors
    The Cambridge Buffs
    The Cambridge Squares
    The Fingerlakes Study Club
    The Florida Everglades
    The Michigan Caprices
    The Tuscan Crowns

Photography by Cromer Studios of Hamilton, Ohio - Photographers, Paul Cromer and Larry Ward.

INTRODUCTION

National Cambridge Collectors, Inc. was incorporated in 1973 as a non-profit educational organization dedicated to the preservation and collection of the products of the Cambridge Glass Company of Cambridge, Ohio. The primary objective of the Organization is to establish and maintain a permanent museum in or near Cambridge for the purpose of display and study of this fine handmade glassware. The museum was opened in 1982.

The Cambridge Glass Company produced fine quality glassware for more than 50 years from 1902 to 1958. During its existence Cambridge produced many thousands of different items and decorations which have become quite collectible. Very few collectors ''collect'' items for the sake of collecting alone. Most collectors are also looking for an enjoyable hobby (or business) with an eye to the future return on the investment being made. Making a good investment is based on knowledge--knowledge of the product and knowledge of its market.

A price guide has been included with this book to serve as a general guide to understanding the market for Cambridge Glass. It must be emphasized that this is only a general guide, as significant regional variations in prices will occur.

There are many factors which distinguish Cambridge Glass from that of other glass manufacturers. These factors include shape, decoration and color. Although shape or decoration alone is frequently adequate to identify an item as a product of the Cambridge Glass Company, all factors must be considered in determining the value of an item. Likewise, an accurate description of all these factors is important in any offer to buy or sell Cambridge Glass. As little as ten years ago it was known that Cambridge produced its wares in at least 35 different colors. Today it is known that the number of colors is closer to 50. The primary purpose of this publication is to make current knowledge of Cambridge colors available to collectors and dealers.

As additional colors have been identified, it has become increasingly difficult to accurately discuss Cambridge colors. Several color names were used for entirely different colors. As a result, collectors have added clarifying adjectives to the Cambridge names. The name Emerald is the best example of this, being used on three different occasions. For example, you will see early dark Emerald, light Emerald and late dark Emerald. Throughout this presentation the generally accepted clarified names are described and used. Similarly, some confusion has been caused by a color name change with no apparent formula change. Examples of these name changes are discussed later.

The presentation sequence of the colors in this book has been designed to further aid the student of Cambridge Glass. In general, the colors are presented in the same sequence as their original introduction by Cambridge. This gives the collector a better ''feel'' for the types of items produced in each color even though not specifically illustrated in that color but shown in contemporary colors. Some colors, such as Ebony, were very long-term colors and the collector should not be surprised by its appearance in just about any shape.

The color names used in this book are the same as those used by Cambridge's sales force. Much of the information and introduction data on the colors was derived from articles and Cambridge advertising in glass trade journals. It has become apparent that not every new color name represented a new color formula. Also, limited company formula (recipe) information indicates that not every formula variation resulted in a new color name. Minor formula variations were made when raw material cost or availability made a change appropriate. Just as with food recipes, there can be more than one glass recipe to achieve the same result. There are also colors, such as Carmen, which used two different formulas, one for blown glass and one for pressed glass. The blown formula was actually darker to provide the same appearance in the thinner blown ware as in the heavier pressed items.

No discussion of Cambridge Glass would be complete without mentioning the manufacturing properties of certain colors. Throughout this text an attempt has been made to discuss those properties which may cause appearance differences. The best example of these differences is found in the Peach-blo color. The ingredients in the Peach-blo formula were prone to darken or burn if overheated. During the process of ''working'' a pot of glass it was necessary to manually adjust the heat. If this were not done precisely, the glass could change color or become poor quality. The tendency of Peach-blo to darken, combined with the name change to Dianthus Pink, has caused many collectors to incorrectly attempt to associate some shades of color with the Peach-blo name and others with Dianthus. An excellent example of the intentional use of such properties can be seen in the color called Rubina. The process of reheating an item in varying amounts from each end produced the color change effect from a single glass formula.

Another important characteristic of some color formulas is the tendency (or lack thereof) to appear darker in thicker sections of glass. This ''gathering'' property can present some problems in color identification. To aid the collector, an attempt has been made in this book to identify those colors which exhibit a tendency to gather the color and appear darker in the thick sections of an item.

Although this book primarily addresses Cambridge colors, some of the color plates present decorative treatments which affect the color appearance (such as carnival) or affect the color name as used by Cambridge. Several plates have been included near the back of the book which present similar colors side by side so that differences can be more clearly illustrated. The final plates show typical examples of the variety of colors which can be accumulated in selective collections.

Note: Throughout the text, marked pieces are noted. Unless otherwise indicated this mark is the small C in a triangle

CONTENTS

OPAL, TURQUOISE, BLUE, GREEN, AMBER

Color production in the early years was not extensive. The first Cambridge catalog issued in 1903 and its associated price list shows novelty items made in Opal, Turquoise, Blue and Amber. Photographers supplies were listed in Green and Amber. The same colors were still listed in a 1906 price list with the exception of Opal and Turquoise which had apparently been discontinued.

Opal is a translucent to opaque white. The white color will vary from a good true white to various degrees of slight grayish or brownish tones. When held to the light the edges will show a good play of opalescence (colors).

Turquoise is a greenish-blue opaque that trends more to the blue than to green.

1903 Blue is a transparent blue of unknown density. There are no confirmed examples of this color.

1903 Amber is a rather lifeless medium deep transparent color.

1903 Green is a deep transparent color with a wide variation in density.

Plate 1 shows examples of the Opal and Turquoise colors in rows 1 and 2. The Royal Blue 4-piece toy tea set in row 2 is a 1916 color which is discussed with plate 2.

Identification of the early transparent colors has been complicated by the lack of distinctive Cambridge molds and limited reference material. Much of the early Cambridge production utilized molds from other glass factories in the National Glass combine. The Amber top hat is believed to be the 1903 Amber. The Green toy tea set and toy mug in row 3 show two different shades from early production. Trade publications issued around 1910 indicate that Cambridge was placing emphasis on special orders and such special orders may account for unusual color variations.

Row 1
1. Opal 8″ Trefoil plate - crosshatch center
2. Opal #130 - 7″ candy plate
3. Opal 8″ Trefoil plate - plain center

Row 2
1. Royal Blue Colonial #2630 4-piece toy tea set
2. Green Colonial #2630 cream and covered sugar
3. Turquoise shaker
4. Opal shaker
5. Turquoise Saratoga hat, toothpick or match box
6. Turquoise 5″ Gem plate

Row 3
1. Green Fernland #2635 4-piece toy tea set - colors do not match
2. Amber Saratoga hat, toothpick or match box
3. Green #136 toy 4 ounce mug - gold flashed ''Mother - 1912''

PLATE 1

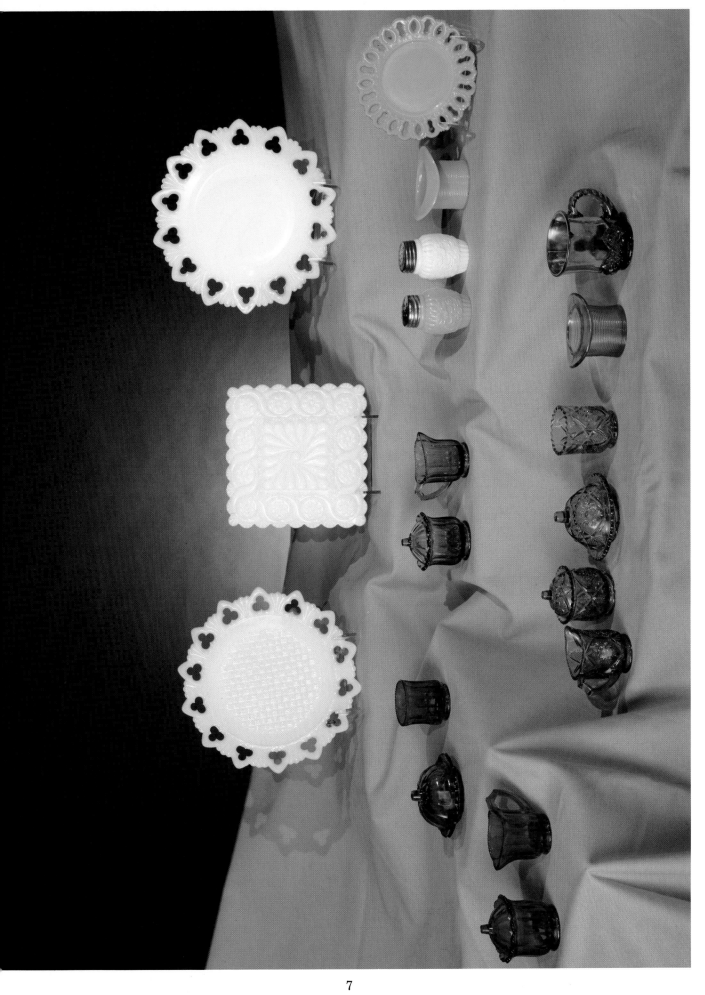

EBONY, ROYAL BLUE, EMERALD, MULBERRY

In January, 1916, Cambridge introduced three new colors: Ebony, Royal Blue and Emerald. A forth color, Mulberry, was introduced in June of the same year. These color names offer much confusion for the Cambridge collector since the names Royal Blue and Mulberry were used again in later years for completely different glass formulas. To make matters worse the name Emerald was used again for *two* other formulas. To reduce confusion the authors recommend that the 1916 colors be referenced as early Royal Blue, early Mulberry and early dark Emerald. The colors of this period can be identified more readily by the shapes in which they are found. With the knowledge that there are always exceptions to the rule, it could be said that "Near Cut" patterns found in one of these hues will be of this time frame.

Ebony is a sparkling black of very high density. It will show color (amethyst, amber or red) when held to a very strong light. Trade journals indicate that Ebony was a very popular color and provided good sales for the company.

An example of early Royal Blue can be seen in Plate 1. It is a medium dark shade of transparent blue. Some trade publications referred to this color as cobalt.

The early dark Emerald is a dark transparent lackluster color. It is mostly found in "Near Cut" patterns and was used as a base glass for the "carnival" treatment.

Early Mulberry is a medium dark amethyst color found more often with "carnival" treatment than plain.

ROW 1
1. Ebony Community #2800/120 16" vase with hand painted enamel flowers
2. Ebony Marjorie #2631 punch bowl, shown with Crystal base
3. Ebony #6018 12" vase with hand painted enamel flowers

ROW 2
1. Ebony Community #2800/124 basket with hand painted enamel flowers
2. Ebony Community #2800 fan vase
3. Ebony #2729 bowl (view of bottom)
4. Ebony Community #2800/125 basket

ROW 3
1. Emerald Thistle #2766 pitcher with gold encrusting - signed NEAR CUT
2. Mulberry #2581 stand lamp
3. Emerald Thistle #2766 bowl - signed NEAR CUT

ROW 4
1. Emerald Strawberry #2780 table tumbler with gold encrusting - signed NEAR CUT
2. Emerald Thistle #2766 cream with gold encrusting - signed NEAR CUT
3. Emerald #2840 7" vase with crimped top
4. Emerald Strawberry #2780 4" nappy - signed NEAR CUT
5. Emerald Thistle #2766 tumbler with gold encrusting - signed NEAR CUT

Note: The "Near Cut" trademark embossed in the glass was introduced in 1905 and was used until about 1920.

PLATE 2

CARNIVAL TREATMENT

"Carnival" is the treatment of hot glass with a spray of metallic salts which produces a very pleasing iridescent effect. Cambridge first used this treatment in 1908 (preceded only by Fenton). It was again used extensively in the 1916-1917 period and possibly in the late 1920s for a third time. It is given a rightful place in this volume due to its color appearance and the fact that much of it required a colored base glass to achieve the beautiful rainbow display of color that resulted.

This treatment is found on most of the major lines of "Near Cut" patterns. It is found in four color classifications:

> Marigold on Crystal glass
> Green on Emerald glass
> Blue on Royal Blue glass
> Purple on Mulberry glass

We have been unable to obtain any Blue pieces for this presentation, but several are known to exist.

ROW 1
1. #2695 cracker jar bottom - on Emerald
2. Marjorie #2631 squat covered cracker jar - on Emerald
3. Feather #2651 cracker jar - on Emerald

ROW 2
1. Strawberry #2780 5½" low comport - signed NEAR CUT - on Mulberry
2. #2666 32 ounce decanter, no stopper - on Emerald
3. Thistle #2766 8¼" bowl (bottom view) - signed NEAR CUT - on Mulberry

ROW 3
1. Strawberry #2780 7" bowl - signed NEAR CUT - on Emerald
2. Buzz Saw #2699/415 8 ounce tumbler - on Crystal
3. Buzz Saw #2699/110 perfume, no stopper - on Emerald
4. Feather #2651 covered butter - signed NEAR CUT - on Mulberry
5. #2351 punch cup - on Crystal
6. Feather #2651 ice cream sundae - on Crystal
7. Sea Shell #34 ash tray - on Crystal (later production, possibly experimental)
8. Strawberry #2780 table tumbler - signed NEAR CUT - on Mulberry

ROW 4
1. Strawberry #2780 table tumbler - signed NEAR CUT - on Crystal
2. Strawberry #2780 flared vase - signed NEAR CUT - on Emerald
3. #2658 tumbler, "Souvenir of Cambridge, Ohio" - on Crystal
4. Strawberry #2780 7" candlestick - on Crystal
5. Strawberry #2780 puff box and cover - on Emerald
6. #2658 cream, "Souvenir of Amana, Iowa" - signed NEAR CUT - on Crystal
7. Strawberry #2780 4" nappy - signed NEAR CUT - on Crystal

PLATE 3

AZURITE

In 1922, Cambridge introduced Azurite which is a light blue opaque that will often show some variation in the color of a given item. Some areas may show streaking that is almost white and other areas may show a little darker color.

The predominance of pieces found in this color will be from the early to mid-1920s production; however, it is known that a few pieces have been found in later production shapes. Perhaps these were only experimental efforts.

Occasionally pieces will be found that have been given either a brown or green enamel spray as a decorative treatment (see Plate 14).

ROW 1
1. Pair #68 10″ candlesticks - black enamel lines decoration
2. Special Article #168 round, handled 10″ sandwich tray with gold decoration
3. Pair 9½″ candlesticks with gold stipple decoration

ROW 2
1. Plainware #1917/256 mayonnaise and underplate
2. Special Article #154 7″ salad plate
3. Top hat, toothpick or match box (top view, see item 5)
4. #2368 10″ paste mold vase
5. Top hat, toothpick or match box (side view, see item 3)
6. Special Article #154 7″ salad plate with gold border
7. Community #2800/237 16 ounce night bottle, tumbler missing

ROW 3
1. Perfume atomizer, gold and black decoration - DeVilbiss sticker
2. Perfume atomizer, gold and black decoration
3. Perfume atomizer, gold and black decoration
4. Plainware #1917/24 cream and sugar
5. Special Article #120 5″ basket
6. Cigarette snuffer for #113 ash tray
7. Special Article #118 8″ basket
8. Special Article #133 3″ x 5″ cigarette box
9. Special Article #132 3″ x 6″ cigarette box
10. Vase/candlestick with gold band
11. Special Article #160 marmalade

ROW 4
1. Tumbler
2. 22 ounce large dog bottle without tumbler top
3. Community #2800/234 soap dish
4. Community #2800/234 ewer and basin with gold edge
5. #2795 3″ toilet box and cover, round
6. #2355 ruffled vase
7. Plainware #1917/87 ½ pound candy jar

PLATE 4

EBONY

Ebony, reintroduced in 1922, is a sparkling black of very high density that will show deep amethyst, red, or shades of brown when held to a strong light. The actual date of production will often be determined by the shape or decoration that was applied. It was apparently carried in the Cambridge line through the late 1940s and probably until the final plant closing.

ROW 1
1. Special Article #151 11″ plate with sterling silver Geisha - signed Rockwell on back
2. 11½″ x 7″ tray with gold encrusted dog
3. #1228 9″ pillow vase with silver encrusted 746 Gloria

ROW 2
1,5 #1228 Scotty dog bookends
2. #1023 9½″ cocktail shaker (lid missing) with D/185 dancing girls
3. Gadroon #3500/45 10″ footed urn vase with gold encrusted Blossom Time
4. Night lamp (in base) with Crystal figure

ROW 3
1. #1626 cigarette lighter
2. Decagon #1090 7″ comport
3. #1041 4½″ swan - signed
4. #1040 3″ swan - signed
5. #1236 ivy ball
6. #70 3½″ turtle flower block
7. Pristine #499 Calla Lily candlestick
8. #1191 6¼″ Cherub candlestick

ROW 4
1. #882 4″ tobacco humidor with red enamel encrusted Dragon
2. Cambridge Square #151 3½″ ash tray
3. #615 cigarette box with silver dog - marked Sterling
4. #388 4″ ash tray with silver dog to match #3 - signed on back
5. #1025 6″ cigar humidor, gold encrusted Hunt Scene
6. Lid only from a #615 small cigarette box, plate etched Adam
7. #607 cigarette box with intalgio dog on cover
8. #3400 ash tray
9. #643 2-piece ash receiver with gold ducks and cattails

PLATE 5

PRIMROSE

Primrose was introduced in 1923 and was a short lived color which was apparently produced for only one or two years.

Primrose is an opaque yellow of considerable warmth and volume. It is of medium depth and not the least extreme in brilliance. Primrose is a very pleasant color in itself and especially attractive with applied decorations. Primrose is frequently confused with Ivory, which is a very pale cream color.

ROW 1
1.   Perfume atomizer, gold and black enamel decoration
2,4 Community #2800/235 7½" candlesticks
3.   Special Article #12 12½" bowl on ebony base
5.   Perfume, no stopper

ROW 2
1.   Special Article #92 11½" stick vase
2.   Special Article #91 10" stick vase
3.   Special Article #90 8" stick vase
4.   Plainware #1917/256 mayonnaise and ladle
5.   Special Article #96 ½ pound candy jar
6.   Pair 9" candlesticks

ROW 3
1.   Special Article #135 10" cheese and cracker with 1" gold border on cracker plate
2.   Small basket
3.   10½" vase with black enamel encrusted Dragon
4.   #2357 6" paste mold vase
5.   Perfume atomizer, black enamel decoration
6.   Special Article #101 5" bonbon and cover with black and gold Greek Key type border

ROW 4
1.   Ring tree
2.   Community #2800/234 sponge bowl with drainer
3.   Community #2800/235 3¾" pin tray - signed with large mark
4.   Community 11½" x 8" vanity tray with #2800/234 covered soap dish, #2800/235 covered pomade jar and #2800/235 covered powder jar
5.   Community #2800/234 brush vase - paper label may not be original

Note: The large trademark (C in a triangle) was introduced about 1921.

PLATE 6

HELIO

Helio, introduced in 1923, is an opaque color of the purple family, delicate in tone and very rich in appearance. A fair amount of variation in depth of color will be found between pieces, but in general, the color is consistent within a given piece. Only occasionally will light color streaking be found.

Helio was a short duration color, probably being in production no more than two years. The name Heliotrope has been used to identify this color but ''Heliotrope'' is not found in any trade references or advertising.

ROW 1
1. Plainware #1917/329 8″ plate with 4½″ seat
2. Special Article #90 8″ stick vase
3. Plainware #1917/361 10½″ center handled sandwich tray
4. #2358 8″ paste mold vase
5. 8″ Laurel Wreath plate

ROW 2
1. #306 3″ paste mold vase
2. Small basket
3,5 #2862 7″ candlesticks
4. Special Article #94 sweet pea vase with platinum edge
6. Perfume atomizer, plate etched 532 with gold encrusting
7. Perfume atomizer, 8 panel
8. Community #2800/234 brush vase

ROW 3
1. Special Article #135 cheese and cracker with gold trim
2. Plainware #1917/415 4½″ plate with 2¾″ seat
3. Special Article #85 10½″ vase with platinum encrusted Classic
4. #2355 10″ vase, ruffled top
5. Cosmetic jar with screw on metal lid
6. #309 6″ vase wtih gold trim
7. #308 4¾″ globe vase

ROW 4
1. Community #2800/235 7½″ candlesticks
2. 3″ vase
3. Vase drilled for lamp with black enamel encrusted Dragon
4. #200/2 7″ candlestick
5. Special Article #101 5″ bonbon and cover

PLATE 7

CARRARA and JADE

In 1923 Cambridge introduced a brilliant, full bodied white opaque called Carrara. It shows considerable opalescence at the edges or in thinner sections when held to a strong light.

The scarcity of representative pieces in this color would indicate that it is the least common of the opaque colors. This color was used in a very limited number of patterns with the Community line being found most often.

ROW 1
1,3 Special Article #65 9½" Doric Column candlesticks
2. Special Article #29 12" bowl with gold encrusted Peacocks

ROW 2
1,5 #200/2 7" candlesticks
2. Feather #2651 item made from goblet mold (Feather was not a regular production line in this time frame)
3. Community #2800/235 3¾" pin tray with gold edge - signed with large mark
4. Community #2800/235 puff box with gold edge

Jade, introduced in 1924, is a medium green opaque having a soft appearance. Shading of the color trends toward the blue side of the spectrum rather than toward the yellow. It will sometimes be found with lighter (almost white) streaking through the piece.

ROW 3
1. Perfume atomizer, gold stippling
2. Perfume, gold stippling
3,5 9½" Doric Column candlesticks
4. 9" footed bowl (Wedgewood style - see note below)
6. 7" perfume atomizer, gold encrusted butterfly and flower decoration.

ROW 4
1. Perfume atomizer, gold bands
2. Special Article #95 1 pound candy jar
3. Special Article #114 6" ash tray
4. Special Article #63 6" Comport
5. Special Article #116 4" ash tray
6. Twist candlestick
7. Perfume lamp globe with black enamel encrusted Dragon
8. #2971 mayonnaise ladle
9. Special Article #90 8" stick vase

Note: This bowl has a smooth top edge, an embossed leaf border around the top, embossed vertical flutings about the body, and handles in the form of ram's heads. It is in the style of the Wedgewood earthenware pattern known as "Belmar."

PLATE 8

TOPAZ

Topaz is another color introduced in 1923. It is a yellow-green transparent color which is often called "vaseline" by many collectors although the correct Cambridge name is Topaz. It is predominately found in shapes of the mid to late 1920s although occasionally found in 1930s shapes such as the #3011 Statuesque line.

ROW 1
1,3   9" twist candlesticks
2.   9½" 14 panel bowl

ROW 2
1.   Everglade #43 12 ounce beer mug
2.   Chelsea #4070/144 ½ pound covered candy
3-5   Weatherford berry set (5 piece)
6.   Stratford #5 2 pint handled jug

ROW 3
1.   8 ounce dog bottle with tumbler cap
2.   Hat ash tray
3.   Beverage urn, plate etched 704 (see note below)
4.   Georgian #319 9 ounce tumbler
5.   #1 Keg set on Ebony tray with 6 barrel glasses - frosted

ROW 4
1.   4-part 2 handled relish, plate etched 732
2.   Pair #227½ candlesticks, plate etched 704
3.   Perfume
4.   Square knobbed powder box
5.   #680 dresser compact with floral cutting
6.   Perfume
7.   Honeycomb 9½" bowl with floral grey cutting - signed

Note: Cambridge is not the only company that made inserts for this type beverage container. The manufacturer can only be determined by the decoration.

PLATE 9

MULBERRY

Mulberry, introduced in 1923, is a medium to deep shade of amethyst in a rather dull transparent color. It will not show the sparkling beauty found in the later issue of Amethyst.

Difficulty will be encountered in distinguishing this color from the earlier Mulberry unless the piece is marked. Items marked with the large triangle C will be the 1923 Mulberry. The correct color of unmarked items can only be determined by knowledge of the production period of the shapes.

ROW 1
1.   9½″ bowl - signed with large mark
2.   #40 10″ flat rim bowl - signed with large mark

ROW 2
1.   Honeycomb 8″ covered candy jar
2.   Plainware #1917/4 sugar with gold encrusting - etching unknown
3.   Night set on tray

ROW 3
1.   Georgian #319 9 ounce tumbler
2.   Honeycomb 4¾″ comport
3.   Plainware #1917/384 5 ounce covered syrup on underplate
4.   Square knobbed powder box
5.   Dome topped powder box

ROW 4
1.   Honeycomb 9½″ bowl - signed with large mark
2.   9½″ 14 panel bowl - signed with large mark

PLATE 10

EMERALD

Emerald is another of the colors introduced in 1923. It is a light transparent shade of green.

Cambridge collectors will often use the name "Light Emerald" as a means of distinguishing between the dark Emerald green of 1916 and the late dark Emerald green of 1949.

The color was used very extensively until the early 1940s. A few of the lines commonly found in Emerald are Weatherford, Round, Decagon and the early styles of figurals such as the Buddha and Geisha.

ROW 1
1,3   8" square optic vases with gold encrusted roses on all 4 panels
2.   10" bowl, plate etched no. 4 with gold encrusting - paper label "22 karat gold"

ROW 2 (entire row etched Hunt Scene)
1.   #3077 6½" plate
2.   10½" decanter with stopper
3.   #3077 12 ounce footed ice tea
4.   Stemmed sherbet
5.   #3077 footed juice
6.   #3077 finger bowl
7.   Round #556 8" plate with gold encrusting - signed

ROW 3
1.   Flower holder (commonly called Melon Boy, believed to be Cambridge but not confirmed)
2.   #1191 Cherub candleholder
3.   Prism sign
4.   #522 two bun Oriental figure (see note below)
5.   #523 one bun Oriental figure (Geisha) on base
6.   #521 large Buddha

ROW 4
1,2   #1160 relish and #1161 dish with gold (part of 5-piece set) - signed
3.   Door knob
4.   #170 9 ounce syrup with metal cover
5.   #2900 5½" small flower ring set
6.   #2900 7" large flower ring set
7.   #2668 2 ounce 2-handled jug
8.   #2675 2 ounce perfume
9.   #701 place card with D/460 gold decoration (in front of item 10)
10.   Weatherford cream and sugar

Note: This plate shows examples of the one bun and two bun Oriental figures. Both of these figures are frequently called Geishas although many believe that the two bun figure may be a representative of a male Oriental figure. The one bun figure was called a Geisha in a 1926 trade advertisement. Without clear evidence of the intended nature of the two bun figure, all references will be simply two bun Oriental figure.

PLATE 11

EMERALD (continued)

ROW 1
1. #977 11″ 2-handled bowl with Nanking Green enamel encrusted 731 - signed
2. Decagon #597 8½″ plate, crackle
3. Martha Washington #4 9″ bowl

ROW 2
1. #881 tumbler, plate etched Golf Scene - from Bridge set
2. #968 cocktail and liner - fruit or seafood - plate etched 731
3. #7606 2 ounce Creme de Menthe - long stem - plate etched Marjorie
4. #3120 9 ounce goblet, plate etched 733
5. #3400/90 8″ 2-part relish, plate etched Gloria
6. #3400/38 12 ounce tumbler, plate etched Diane
7. #1203 7 ounce shammed whiskey with silver decorated fighting cocks - signed Rockwell

ROW 3
1. Dresser compact with gold encrusted flowers and Peach-blo rose knob
2-4 #510 console set with Temple jar etched Blue Willow and Dolphin candlesticks
5. 1 pound candy jar with Peach-blo rose knob

ROW 4
1. #300 6″ 3-footed candy box, plate etched no. 4
2. #2374 11″ vase, plate etched Windsor with gold border and gold on foot
3. Mount Vernon #1340 2½ ounce cologne
4. Meat platter and gravy boat, plate etched 732
5. #3400/79 6 ounce oil
6. #643 2-piece ash receiver
7. #2366 12″ vase, plate etched 724

PLATE 12

IVORY

Introduction of the successful opaque colors continued in 1924 with the introduction of Ivory. It is a light cream opaque very similar to the material from which its name was derived. Colors of this hue by Cambridge and other companies are commonly called ''Custard'' but the correct Cambridge name is Ivory.

The light hue of this color made it an ideal background base for many of the applied decorations of this time period. See plate 14 for additional examples of special treatments applied to Ivory and other opaques.

ROW 1
1. Large bitters bottle
2. #6004 8″ vase, gold encrusted basket of flowers with gold edge
3. Special Article #94 7″ sweet pea vase
4. Perfume atomizer, enameled basket of flowers
5. #174 9 ounce syrup pitcher with metal top

ROW 2
1. Special Article #248 10″ low footed comport
2. Weatherford berry bowl
3. #523 one bun Oriental figure (Geisha)
4. Special Aritcle #91 10″ stick vase with enamel floral decoration
5. Special Article #39 11½″ bowl with enamel and gold decoration

ROW 3
1. Perfume atomizer, black and gold band decoration
2. 8½″ perfume atomizer, blue enamel decoration
3. #680 dresser compact, enameled Iris decoration
4. Perfume, enameled Iris decoration
5. Perfume, enameled floral decoration

ROW 4 (entire row blue enamel encrusted Blue Willow)
1. Round #559 8½″ salad plate
2. Round #494 footed cup and saucer
3. 3-footed covered candy box
4. Special Article #34 10″ bowl
5. Special Article #95 ½ pound covered candy jar

PLATE 13

SPECIAL TREATMENTS

This plate has been included to illustrate how special treatments or decorations can change an item's color appearance. Color treatments can easily be mistaken for colored glass. Examine suspected items carefully on edges and around the bottom for untreated or thinly treated areas which reveal the base glass.

ROW 1
1,3   Dolphin candlesticks - Ivory with caramel flashing
2.   Martha Washington #7 12½" bowl - Crystal with gold flashing

ROW 2
1.   13½" owl lamp - Ivory with brown enamel, with Ebony base
2.   #1043 8½" swan - Ebony with satin finish, coral red enameled head
3.   10½" monkey lamp - Ivory with brown enamel, with Ebony base

ROW 3
1.   Special Article #71 Azurite candlesticks with gold trim, green enamel on base
2.   Special Article #57 Azurite 8¼" footed bowl, purple iridescence on outside - signed triangle C in black enamel
3.   Helio 3-footed 6" bowl with gold decoration on edge - iridescence on outside
4.   Special Article #83 Ivory 8" vase with black enamel and daisy decoration - iridescence below decoration

PLATE 14

AMBER and MADEIRA

Amber is a deep brown tone in a transparent color. It was first mentioned in Cambridge company literature and the glass trade publications in January, 1924, using the name "Amber," but it also had other names during the next few years. In April of 1926 the Company advertising started using the name "Amber-glo."

During the mid 1930s, the name "Almond" was applied to pieces of Amber that had been given a special treatment. These pieces were acid treated for a satin finish on one side and untreated on the other. See plate 22 for a similar treatment of Amber glass called "Cinnamon."

Madeira was introduced in June, 1929, and was advertised for about one year. It was described as a light golden shade, halfway between canary yellow and deep amber.

ROW 1
1. #880/881 5-piece bridge set, plate etched Hunt Scene (Madeira)
2. #3400/95 4½" puff box
3. #520 small Buddha
4. Sea Shell #44 6" flower center
5. #1393 cocktail mixer

ROW 2
1. Tally-Ho #1402/100 Crystal wine with Amber stem
2,3,5 #3400/647 candlesticks with #3400/4 center bowl - all gold encrusted Wildflower
4. Prism sign
6. #3400/40 sugar shaker

ROW 3
1. Salad fork and spoon (across front)
2. #2366 12" vase, plate etched 724
3. Plainware #1917/138 sugar and cream, plate etched Blue Willow
4. Weatherford covered syrup
5. Everglade #32 1-lite candlestick
6. Everglade #38 11" footed vase

ROW 4 (all Mount Vernon pattern)
1. #8 cream and sugar
2. #84 14 ounce handled stein - signed
3. #66 cigarette holder on #1066 Aurora stem
4. #102 oval 2-handled salt dip (also Stratford #103)
5. #22 3 ounce footed tumbler
6. #29 2½ ounce mustard
7. #18 7 ounce toilet bottle
8. #5 8½" salad plate with #7 cup and saucer - signed

PLATE 15

AMBER and MADEIRA (continued)

ROW 1
1. Sea Shell #42 7½" shell flower center - paper label
2. #3400/14 7" tall comport, plate etched Diane
3. Caprice #339 8" vase

ROW 2
1. #3400/50 square 4-toed cup and saucer, plate etched Apple Blossom, signed
2. ½ pound candy jar
3. Decagon #1235 9½" bowl, plate etched grapes and leaves - signed
4. Honeycomb covered candy jar
5. Tally-Ho #1402/35 12 ounce handled stein

ROW 3
1. #1315 5" rabbit box with satin finish
2. #1222 turkey
3. #1043 8½" swan - signed

ROW 4
1. #680 dresser compact with ornate metal filigree lid
2. Temple jar (part of #510 console set), no lid, D/185 - paper label ''22 karat gold''
3. Lexington #2860 2-handled berry sugar
4. #701 place card (in front of sugar)
5. Laurel Wreath 6¼" plate - signed (Madeira)
6. #3400/18 shaker
7. Top hat cigarette holder

PLATE 16

COBALT BLUE 1

Cobalt Blue 1 is the first of two little known cobalt blue colors of the 1920s. The name Cobalt Blue 1 has been adopted by collectors since the actual name used by Cambridge has not been determined. Extremely limited evidence suggests that the name AURORA may have been used. Researchers have not been able to determine the exact date of introduction for Cobalt Blue 1. The items seen in this color frequently appear in other colors associated with the early to mid 1920s. The earliest known reference to a cobalt glass in this time period occurred in a trade article in April, 1924. None of the trade references in 1924 suggest that it was a new color. Whether introduced in 1924 or earlier, it's production life was short.

Cobalt Blue 1 is a medium blue. It is the lightest of the two cobalts of the 1920s and can usually be distinguished from the other with the naked eye. Cobalt Blue 1 exhibits a significant "gathering effect" and appears much darker in thick sections of glass. Under black light, Cobalt Blue 1 is highly florescent whereas the other cobalt shows little or no florescence.

Not many of the items found in Cobalt Blue 1 are signed. When signed, the large triangle C was used.

ROW 1
1.   Perfume, gold encrusted Adam
2.   Beverage urn, plate etched Martha
3.   Chelsea #4070/61 4¼" berry bowl with frosted edge

ROW 2
1.   14 panel bowl
2.   Plainware #1917/88 ½ pound candy jar
3.   9½" bowl - signed

ROW 3
1.   Plainware #1917/4 cream
2.   Night set and tray with floral grey cutting
3.   14 panel bowl

PLATE 17

RUBINA

Our first reference to the name Rubina appears in an advertisement from January 12, 1925. It was a very short term color.

Rubina is a multicolor presentation that will shade from a red at the top and bottom of an item into a green and then to a rich medium blue in the middle. Due to the hand operation involved in the reheating process, there may be variation in the intensity of the colors derived. In some circumstances the blue and green shades have completely disappeared leaving only the red. Note particularly the 8½" candlesticks in row 3.

ROW 1
1. 10¼" block optic vase
2. #1630 12 ounce tumbler, no optic
3. Block optic covered pitcher
4. Block optic tumbler
5. 10¼" vase, block optic bottom

ROW 2
1,3 9½" Doric Column candlesticks
2. 9" footed bowl with ram's head handles

ROW 3
1. Honeycomb squat covered candy jar
2. 8½" candlestick
3. 8½" candlestick
4. 8½" candlestick
5. Honeycomb 10" bowl - signed with large mark

ROW 4
1. Honeycomb comport
2. Honeycomb 6" bowl - signed with large mark
3. Honeycomb 9" low footed comport 4¾" tall
4. #118 8" basket

PLATE 18

RUBINA (continued)

ROW 1
1. Honeycomb 4″ low comport
2. Candy jar - signed with large mark
3. 6½″ tall comport - signed with large mark

ROW 2
1,3 Dolphin candlesticks
2. Special Article #94 7″ sweet pea vase

ROW 3
1. Georgian #319 9 ounce tumbler
2. 7½″ candlesticks, pair
3. Narrow optic goblet
4. Narrow optic juice

ROW 4
1. Mayonnaise and ladle
2. 10″ bowl with sponge acid treatment on outside
3. 5 ounce juice
4. Handled ice tea - signed with large mark

PLATE 19

PEACH-BLO / DIANTHUS PINK

Peach-blo is a soft pink with warmth and sparkle. It was first advertised in August, 1925. Pink is a very hard color to maintain while working a pot of glass and tends to have a considerable amount of variation in density and sparkle. The time period in which a blank was manufactured will often determine the correct color name. In 1934 the color name was changed to Dianthus Pink with no apparent formula change.

As with many other manufacturers, Cambridge used colors in combination (see row 3). This trend was especially popular in the late 1920s when Peach-blo was at its peak.

ROW 1
1. #2824 Pansy berry cream and sugar - signed NEAR CUT
2. Optic window vase, plate etched Cleo
3. Covered cracker jar, plate etched Hunt Scene
4. #620 cream and sugar, plate etched Marjorie - sugar signed

ROW 2
1. #3115 5 ounce footed tumbler, plate etched 731 with Willow Blue foot
2. Aero Optic #880/8701 5-piece bridge set with card suit symbols molded in tray
3. 10" 2-handled bowl, plate etched 732 with gold decoration
4. #2746 cigar or tobacco jar
5. #1196 bathroom bottle, acid etched "Cotton"

ROW 3
1. #1315 5" rabbit box
2. #518 8½" flower center
3. Wine, plate etched Hunt Scene, with light Emerald foot
4. Sani-shaving service, patent no. 75,445
5. Prism sign
6. Perfume, gold encrusted etching no. 4
7. Candleholder insert to fit 4½" swan
8. #3300 banana split

ROW 4
1. #1110 dessert mold with satin finish
2. Decagon #597 8-3/8" salad plate, crackle
3. Round #925 After Dinner cup and saucer - cup signed
4. #3400/130 11 ounce tumbler
5,6 #512 rose lady flower center and #823 square flower center with candle cups, floral etching with gold
7. #3400/69 After Dinner cup and saucer, plate etched Gloria
8. Decagon #811 9½" dinner plate, etched Cleo
9. Round #960 cream and sugar, plate etched Cleo

PLATE 20

COBALT BLUE 2 and RITZ BLUE

These two colors are so close in appearance that it is frequently impossible to distinguish between them. Ritz Blue is slightly darker and more evenly colored than Cobalt Blue 2 which displays a significant gathering effect. Natural sunlight provides the best lighting condition to observe the difference between them while incandescent lighting is the worst. Cobalt Blue 2 shows a slight florescence under black light while Ritz Blue shows absolutely none.

Cobalt Blue 2, as collectors have named it, was introduced in January, 1925. There is very limited evidence, that it may have been called NIGHT BLUE by Cambridge. Trade references to cobalt continue through 1925 into 1926. Cobalt Blue 2 was probably discontinued when Bluebell was introduced in the summer of 1926.

The production dates for Ritz Blue are more elusive. There are no applicable trade references. Ritz Blue is commonly seen in Decagon which was introduced as a full line in 1928 and continued into the early 1930s. The name Ritz Blue first appeared in a Cambridge internal letter date November 23, 1929. It also appears in a January, 1931, advertisement.

All items shown are Cobalt Blue 2 except as noted.

ROW 1
1. Honeycomb comport - signed
2. Square knobbed powder box
3. Decagon #815 7½″ plate - signed - Ritz Blue
4. #189 perfume with gold encrusted etching no.4
5. Round #254 5½″ comport

ROW 2
1. #1 Keg set
2. Decagon #1076 cream and sugar - Ritz Blue
3. Beverage urn, plate etched 695

ROW 3
1. Candy jar, optic
2. Plainware #1917/88 1 pound candy jar, optic, with grey cutting - Ritz Blue
3. #2366 12″ vase with gold encrusted Classic
4. #189 perfume
5. Pair 8¼″ candlesticks

ROW 4
1,3 Dolphin candlesticks
2. #520 Buddha

PLATE 21

BLUEBELL

Bluebell was first mentioned in a glass trade publication article of August 30, 1926. This medium dark transparent color has a rich full bodied beauty with considerable sparkle. Thicker items in this color appear darker. Note the darker appearance of the Oriental figure in row 1 and the lighter appearance of the tray below it.

The shapes used with this color indicate that it was used only for a short period of time. On this page the Cascade goblet seems to be an exception to the rule and indicates that the color was attempted again at a later date. The Cascade line was not introduced until 1947.

In the 1940s Cambridge advertised Harlequin sets with eight colors (see color plate 56) that included the color Tahoe blue which cannot be easily distinguished from Bluebell.

ROW 1
1.   #522 two bun Oriental figure
2.   #463 Dolphin handled bowl
3.   #518 8½" flower holder

ROW 2
1.   #397 celery and relish tray
2,4   Round #138 cream and sugar, plate etched Blue Willow with gold band trim
3.   #3077 6 ounce tall sherbet, plate etched 731
5.   4-footed oval bowl 13" x 8½"

ROW 3
1.   #1070 pinched decanter
2.   Perfume, plate etched 704, with gold
3.   Powder box, plate etched 704, with partial gold fill
4.   Twisted optic covered Temple jar
5.   Prism sign
6.   Perfume with beehive stopper
7.   #1222 turkey
8.   Cascade #4000/1 goblet

ROW 4
1.   Georgian #319 9 ounce tumbler
2.   Round #912 casserole and cover with gold encrusted floral decoration
3.   #1066 2½ ounce tumbler
4.   Plainware #1917/361 10" sandwich tray
5.   #2906 5¼" low comport

PLATE 22

WILLOW BLUE / ELEANOR BLUE

In August, 1928, Cambridge introduced a light pastel called Willow Blue. When introduced, it was described as ''sky blue, very transparent.'' It has no bunching of color and remains uniform in appearance regardless of the thickness of the glass.

Often confused with Moonlight blue, Willow Blue can also be identified by the shapes in which it is found. Decagon and Round are lines commonly found in Willow Blue.

Research indicates that the name was changed to ''Eleanor Blue'' between May and October, 1933.

ROW 1
1,3   #1155 candlesticks
2.   Everglade #40 6″ comport

ROW 2
1.   #3400/158 11½″ cocktail shaker with grey cutting
2.   #274 10″ vase, plate etched 724 with gold edge
3.   #3077/10 63 ounce jug and cover, plate etched 742

ROW 3
1,2   Decagon #758/759 mayonnaise and underplate with unknown cutting - signed
3.   Decagon #1095 3-piece sugar and cream set
4.   #3400/71 3″ 4-footed nut cup - signed
5.   #3300 sherbet
6.   #3400/94 3½″ puff box, plate etched Portia
7.   Decagon #801 10 ounce goblet, plate etched Cleo

ROW 4
1,3   Leaf line #1211 6″ candelabrum
2.   Leaf line #1207 11″ center bowl

PLATE 23

MYSTIC, CINNAMON, ROSE du BARRY, JADE, KRYSTOL

February, 1930, saw the introduction of a complete set of new color names. Technically they were not new colors, but only treatments applied to existing colors. These were acid treatments that were applied in a manner that "frosted" the background and highlighted the motif in a bright (not frosted) effect. Only the pattern side of the glass was frosted. This was called "Springtime" and these color names apply only to this line.

The following were the names used and the actual color used:

> Mystic - used Willow Blue glass
> Cinnamon - used Amber glass
> Rose du Barry - used Peach-blo glass (no examples shown)
> Jade - used light Emerald glass
> Krystol - used Crystal glass (no examples shown)

ROW 1 (Cinnamon)
1,3   Pair #646 5" candlesticks, commonly called ring stem
2.   #512 rose lady flower center on old style base

ROW 2 (Cinnamon)
1,3   #1155 1-lite candlesticks
2.   #1125 16" bowl, fancy rolled edge (depicts buffalo hunt scene)

ROW 3
1.   Jade #1253 12" vase
2.   Mystic Blue #1125 16" bowl, fancy rolled edge
3.   Jade 3-footed nappy

PLATE 24

GOLD KRYSTOL

Gold Krystol was introduced to the trade August 26, 1929. It is light yellow with no amber tint. This transparent color is similar to Willow Blue in that the color does not bunch or collect in the heavier areas of the glass.

ROW 1
1.   Mount Vernon #84 14 ounce stein - signed
2,4   #646 5″ candlesticks
3.   #1322 26 ounce decanter, plate etched Gloria
5.   #3400/9 7″ candy box and cover, gold encrusted Gloria

ROW 2
1.   #3077 12 ounce footed tumbler, plate etched Cleo
2.   #3120 12 ounce footed tumbler, plate etched 739
3.   #3130 goblet, plate etched Apple Blossom
4.   #3025 10 ounce goblet, plate etched Gloria, with Amber stem and foot

ROW 3
1.   #3400/68 cream and sugar - sugar signed
2.   #3400/9 7″ candy box and cover, plate etched Apple Blossom
3.   #1312 footed cigarette box and cover, plate etched Diane
4.   #1704 5″ hat

ROW 4
1.   #3400/83 square After Dinner cup and saucer - signed
2.   #3400/70 3½″ cranberry, plate etched Apple Blossom
3.   #3400/2 12½″ bowl, fancy rolled edge, etched Apple Blossom - signed
4.   #3400/97 2 ounce perfume, optic, in ornate metal filigree holder
5.   #1040 3″ swan - signed

PLATE 25

AVOCADO

Avocado is a rich green opaque that tends toward the yellow side of the green spectrum. The name "Avocado" has been affixed to this color by collectors of Cambridge glass. No reference to the name has been found in any trade publication or company literature. The shapes found lead us to believe that it had limited production in the 1927-28 time period.

ROW 1
1. #173 12" sandwich tray, oval
2. Goblet, gold encrusted Hunt Scene
3. #639 4" candlestick with ornate silver decoration
4. Special Article #39 11½" bowl, flat rim

ROW 2
1,3 9" candlesticks
2. #732 Refectory bowl with gold encrusted floral decoration

ROW 3
1. Plainware #1917/20 6 ounce cream and sugar
2. #2746 cigar or tobacco jar, without lid
3. Desk set - ridged holder for pens and pencils, letter holder, pin holder, pair bookends

ROW 4 (all items are Round line)
1. #901 12½" oval service tray with 9½" pitcher and #394 ice tub
2. #556 8" salad plate
3. #466 6" cereal or grapefruit
4. #810 9½" dinner plate
5. #933 cup and saucer

PLATE 26

CARMEN

Carmen, a rich full bodied red, was introduced in February, 1931, to start a new trend of dark transparent colors. Although there is some range in the density of the color, Carmen does not bear the depth of color or hardness of appearance that is often found in the ruby colors of other glass companies.

Color variations toward yellow will be found in some items. This is sometimes described as "Amberina" but no reference has been found indicating that Cambridge ever used the name Amberina. It is reasonable to conclude that any pieces with this yellow trend should still be called Carmen.

ROW 1
1,3 Statuesque #3011/61 candlesticks with bobeches and prisms
2. Statuesque #3011/40 10″ flower center, frequently called a flying lady bowl

ROW 2
1. #3400/4 12″ 4-footed bowl with Japonica decoration - signed Japonica
2. #3400/93 5½″ ivy ball with Japonica decoration
3. #1242 10″ vase with Japonica decoration - signed Japonica

ROW 3
1. 14½″ lamp with gold encrusted Diane (made from a #1301 vase)
2. #3400/62 8½″ salad plate with gold encrusted Portia
3. #3035 6 ounce tall sherbet with gold encrusted Portia
4. #3035 3 ounce cocktail with gold encrusted Portia
5. #3400/102 5″ globe vase with gold encrusted Portia - signed

ROW 4
1. Tally-Ho #1402/76 5″ candlesticks
2. Tally-Ho #1402/101/102 17½″ cheese and cracker
3. Tally-Ho #1402/49 88 ounce jug with Crystal handle

Note: Japonica is an unusual white enamel decoration depicting an Oriental flowering shrub. It has been seen on Carmen, Royal Blue, Forest Green and Amethyst. Before applying the enamel, most blanks were frosted on one side and left bright on the other. Many Japonica items carry a special white enamel trademark shown below.

PLATE 27

CARMEN (continued)

ROW 1
1. #1305 10″ ring stem vase
2. Sea Shell #44 6″ flower center
3. #119 7″ handled basket with Carmen handle

ROW 2
1. Pressed Rose Point goblet
2. #1321 28 ounce decanter and 4 #7966 2 ounce sherries with silver grapes and leaves
3. #3400/90 8″ 2-part relish with ornate silver decoration

ROW 3 (entire row is silk screen decorated)
1. #3400/92 32 ounce ball shaped decanter with gold Bordeaux decoration
2. #3500 1 ounce cordial with gold basket decoration
3. #3500 5 ounce footed tumbler with gold basket decoration
4. #3400/98 ball shaped cream and sugar with gold Bordeaux decoration
5. #3500 finger bowl with gold basket decoration - same as #2 and #3
6. Tally-Ho #1402/100 cocktail with gold decoration D/1007
7. Tally-Ho #1402/87 covered cookie or pretzel jar, without handle, with gold decoration D/1007

ROW 4
1. #1312 footed cigarette box and cover
2,4 #3400/646 candlesticks, gold encrusted Rose Point
3. #3400/4 12″ 4-footed bowl, gold encrusted Rose Point
5. #1314 ash tray

PLATE 28

CARMEN (continued)

ROW 1
1. Cascade #4000/1 goblet
2. #1405 16 ounce beer mug
3. #1701 9″ hat
4. #3400/103 6½″ vase, aero optic style

ROW 2
1. Mount Vernon 3-piece toilet set - two #18 7 ounce toilet bottles, one #17 4″ toilet box - box signed
2. Pristine #578 miniature cornucopia
3. Leaf line #1216 candelabrum with flower holder
4. Statuesque #3011/25 ivy ball
5. #3078 2½ ounce tumbler
6. #3078 wine

ROW 3
1. #3130 9 ounce goblet, plate etched 731
2. Tally-Ho #1402/47 4″ coaster
3. #3400/141 80 ounce jug
4. Nautilus #3450/1130 11″ vase - color very dark
5. #1206 76 ounce Twisted Optic pitcher, ice lipped
6. #3400/76 salt and pepper with glass tops
7. Gadroon #3500/90 cigarette holder with ash tray foot

ROW 4
1. Martha Washington #20 6-3/8″ bread and butter plate
2. #3400/54 cup and saucer
3. #3400/52 5½″ butter and cover
4,6 Sonata #1957/121 candlesticks
5. #19 Bobeche
7. Night set on tray - NOTE: not correct Cambridge tumbler for this set

PLATE 29

AMETHYST

Amethyst was described in the February, 1931, introductory trade articles as "a burgundy or deep amethyst." This very rich color, although quite deep in tone, is typical of the softness of appearance that exemplifies the darker colors of Cambridge.

A treatment sometimes applied to this color was the frosted or satin finish. When this process was applied to one side of the blank only with the other remaining bright, the color was called "Grape." The name Grape was first mentioned in advertising literature in April, 1935.

ROW 1
1. #1337 cigarette holder with ash tray foot
2. Nautilus #3450 cream and sugar
3. Nautilus #3450 salt and pepper on Crystal handled tray (3-piece set) with "Canadian Club" white enamel silk screened on sides
4. #1066 oval cigarette holder with ash tray foot

ROW 2
1. Caprice #340 9" vase
2. #274 10" bud vase, gold encrusted Elaine
3. Tally-Ho #1402/44 15 ounce tumbler
4. #1369 36 ounce Melon fluted decanter
5. Sea Shell #42 8" flower center

ROW 3
1. #3400/69 After Dinner cup and saucer - both signed
2,4 Statuesque #3011/60 candlesticks
3. Sea Shell #40 10½" flying lady bowl
5. Gadroon #3500/79 3" basket

ROW 4
1. #1236 7½" ring stem footed ivy ball
2. Tally-Ho #1402/139 10" top hat
3. #1330 5" Sweet Potato vase
4. #1 2½" star candleholder
5. #1431 8" bulb vase

PLATE 30

ROYAL BLUE

Royal Blue, introduced in June, 1931, was used extensively throughout the 1930s and into the 1940s. This color was apparently dropped from production during World War II due to the scarcity of raw materials.

It is a deep color of transparent blue with a pleasant softness that will show highlights trending toward the reds. The striking beauty of this rich color creates a desirability level among collectors that favorably affects prices.

ROW 1
1.   #1070 36 ounce pinched decanter with golf ball stopper
2.   Decagon #842 12″ bowl - signed
3.   Tally-Ho #1402/39 34 ounce squat decanter with stopper

ROW 2
1.   #3400/46 12 ounce cabinet flask
2.   Round #925 After Dinner cup and saucer, gold inside cup and on handle - signed
3.   Gadroon #3500/109 11″ 4-toed ram's head bowl
4.   Mount Vernon #29 2½ ounce mustard
5.   Mount Vernon #66 cigarette holder with ash tray foot on #1066 stem - paper label
6.   Mount Vernon #84 14 ounce stein - signed

ROW 3
1.   #1242 10″ vase gold encrusted Gloria
2.   Special Article #86 8″ vase with a silver parrot decoration
3.   Prism sign with gold encrusted ''Cambridge Glass''
4.   #1302 9″ vase on ring stem, Japonica decoration
5.   #1206 12 ounce spiral narrow optic tumbler - paper label
6.   Tally-Ho #1402/51 15″ handled cocktail shaker with #5 chromium plated top

ROW 4
1,3 Gadroon #3500/74 4½″ candlesticks with ram's heads
2.   Gadroon #3500/25 9″ bowl, ram's head

PLATE 31

ROYAL BLUE (continued)

ROW 1
1. #3400/93 5½″ ivy ball with gold encrusted Bordeaux
2. #3400/154 76 ounce pinched jug
3. #3400/1338 3-lite candlestick

ROW 2
1. #1238 12″ vase with Japonica decoration
2-6 Caprice #187 decanter with stopper in Farber holder and four #188 2 ounce tumblers
7. #3078 32 ounce decanter with stopper - paper label

ROW 3
1,3 #646 5″ candlesticks with Decagon base gold encrusted D/995 Chintz with gold edge
2. #3400/4 12″ 4-footed bowl gold encrusted D/995 Chintz

ROW 4
1. Pressed Rose Point sherbet
2. Pressed Rose Point cocktail
3. #3400/92 32 ounce decanter with sterling decoration of tavern drinking scene - signed Sterling
4. #3400/144 cigarette holder with ash tray foot and place card holder
5. Gadroon #3500/41 10″ covered urn
6. Pair #628 3½″ candlesticks with Japonica decoration

PLATE 32

FOREST GREEN

Forest Green was introduced in September, 1931. It is a soft, cool, dark shade of transparent green that tends toward yellow.

Forest Green is often confused with the dark Emerald color of the later period of production (see row 3, item 3).

In April, 1935, a decorative treatment was introduced that combined a bright finish on one side of the ware with a matte (frosted) finish on the other side. When applied to Forest Green pieces, the color was called "Jade Green."

ROW 1
1. #1352 handled frog vase with detail
2. #1352 handled frog vase without detail
3. #1403 10 ounce pilsner
4. #119 7″ basket with Crystal handle
5. #3400/132 9″ vase

ROW 2
1. Tally-Ho #1402/5 7½ ounce tall sherbet with gold silk screen decoration
2. Tally-Ho #1402/44 15 ounce tumbler with gold silk screen decoration
3. Everglade #26 sugar
4. #3400/103 6½″ globe vase, satin finish outside and inside, with Japonica decoration
5. Everglade #24 sherbet
6. Martha #163 8½″ Asparagus plate

ROW 3
1. #1203 5 ounce tumbler, plate etched 401 Old Fashioned Grape - signed
2. Tally-Ho #1402/100 comport
3. #1633 peg vase for Cambridge Arms (color is late dark Emerald, not Forest Green)
4. #1446 6″ vase, aero optic style
5. Martha Washington #67 covered pretzel jar - paper label
6. Mount Vernon #12 4½″ footed ivy ball
7. #3400/99 6 ounce oil, gold encrusted Bordeaux
8. Cigarette holder with ash tray foot
9. #3103 12 ounce footed tumbler - Forest Green stem only
10. #496 2½ ounce shammed tumbler, cut flute, plate etched 401 Old Fashioned Grape

ROW 4
1. #595 12 ounce beer stein
2. #3400/107 pitcher, plate etched Portia
3. #1 4½″ twist muddler
4. 10¾″ high 2-piece flower pot - paper label - 11½″ across top
5. #1239 14″ ring stem vase, plate etched Valencia
6. #2 4″ star candleholder
7. Tally-Ho #1402/35 12 ounce handled stein

PLATE 33

HEATHERBLOOM

Heatherbloom was introduced in November, 1931, and the last advertising reference to the color was found in 1935.

This color can be deceiving. When viewed in natural light (daylight or incandescent) it is a very delicate pale orchid or lavender. When viewed under fluorescent light, it generally takes on a light blue or gray appearance. In general, the fact that it is a changeable color helps in making a positive identification. There have been a few items found which do not change color. Most of these exception items are signed and, therefore, are not a problem.

Caution! This color could be confused with Crystal which has changed to a lavender shade by prolonged exposure to sunlight.

ROW 1 (all items are Mount Vernon)
1.   #84 stein
2.   #12 4½" ivy ball
3.   #50 6" flared vase
4.   #34 6" comport, twist stem
5.   #8 cream

ROW 2
1.   #3035 10 ounce footed tumbler, plate etched 731
2.   #3400/68 sugar, plate etched Gloria - signed
3.   #3122 9 ounce goblet, plate etched Diane
4.   #3400/176 7½" salad plate, plate etched Diane
5.   #3400/97 2 ounce ball shaped perfume, plate etched Portia, with dropper stopper
6.   #3126 7 ounce tall sherbet, plate etched Portia
7.   #3400/38 12 ounce tumbler, plate etched Portia
8.   #3126 9 ounce goblet, plate etched Portia

ROW 3
1.   Pair Mount Vernon #38 13½" candelabrum

ROW 4
1.   Martha Washington #41 9½" urn
2.   #496 2½ ounce shot glass, cut flute
3.   #3121 6 ounce tall sherbet, all Heatherbloom (more frequently seen with Crystal stem and foot)
4.   #3400/99 6 ounce oil, twist optic
5.   Statuesque #3011/13 1 ounce brandy
6.   #3400/68 cream and sugar - signed
7.   #3400/71 3" 4-toed nut cup - signed
8.   Pair #646 5" candlesticks with Decagon base

PLATE 34

CROWN TUSCAN

Crown Tuscan was introduced in September, 1932, and was continued until the closing of the Company.

It is a pinkish color that will range from near translucent to opaque in density and is sometimes described as being "near flesh color."

It is found in a wide range of shades from a dark tan through shades of pink to almost white. Some pieces show streaks that approach brown in a slag effect. It is a color that accepts a very high degree of fire polishing which could result in a show of opalescence near the edges.

ROW 1
1. Gadroon #3500/42 12" urn with "Cambridge Glass" in gold
2. #1300 8" vase, gold encrusted Rose Point
3. Gadroon #3500/42 12" urn, gold encrusted Portia

ROW 2
1. #1337 cigarette holder on Ebony ash tray foot
2,4 #1307 3-lite candlesticks, gold encrusted D/995 Chintz - Crown Tuscan signature
3. #3400/102 5" globe vase, gold encrusted D/995 Chintz - Crown Tuscan signature
5. #1283 8" vase with Ebony foot

ROW 3
1. #1253 12" vase - paper label
2. 18" Mannequin head
3. #3400/152 76 ounce Doulton jug

An actual Crown Tuscan signature is reproduced below:

TUSCAN

U.S.A.

PLATE 35

CROWN TUSCAN (continued)

ROW 1
1-3 #1321 28 ounce decanter with two #7966 2 ounce sherries
4.   #274 10″ vase with "Charleton" decoration
5.   #2355 epergne vase
6.   #1321 28 ounce decanter, gold encrusted Portia - Crown Tuscan signature

ROW 2
1.   Everglade #21 7½″ vase
2.   #1043 8½″ swan with "Charleton" decoration
3.   #1307 3-lite candelabra with gold - Crown Tuscan signature

ROW 3
1.   Nautilus #3450 40 ounce decanter
2.   Gadroon #3500/57 8″ 3-part covered candy box with "Charleton" decoration
3.   Nautilus #3450 28 ounce decanter

ROW 4
1.   Cascade #4000/671 ice bucket
2.   #2899 3″ flower block
3.   #3400/4 12″ 4-toed bowl with "Charleton" decoration
4.   #1506/1 4″ novelty basket
5.   #3400/114 64 ounce ball shaped jug

Note: "Charleton" is the registered trademark for a class of hand decorations done by Abels, Wasserberg & Co., Inc. of New York.

PLATE 36

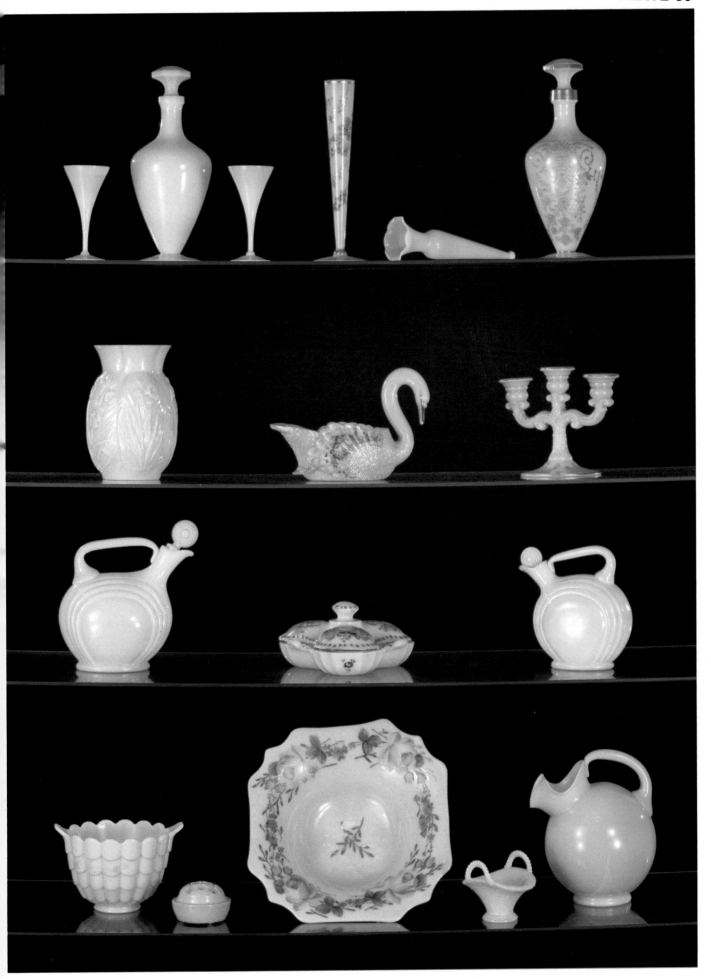

CORAL

Coral was introduced in February, 1935, as one of the colors of the Sea Shell line. No substantial evidence has been found to indicate that this was a distinct color formula. It is probable that this color name was coined by the sales department of the Company as being a more appropriate name to apply to Crown Tuscan when used in the "Sea Shell" line.

When the Sea Shell line was introduced, one author described the Coral color as a "shade with a tinting of coral on bluish white." He was describing the blue opalescent appearance of the thinner sections characteristic of some items in the Sea Shell line (see row 3, item 3). This has lead some collectors to debate whether Coral was a unique color formula. Nevertheless, the name Coral was not used outside the Sea Shell line. The Crown Tuscan name was not applied to the Sea Shell line until 1949 when Cambridge had stopped using the Coral name and used the Crown Tuscan name on all lines.

ROW 1
1,3 Sea Shell #61 candlesticks made for bobeches and prisms (also #3011 Statuesque line)
2. Sea Shell #40 10½" flower or fruit center with "Charleton" decoration

ROW 2
1. Sea Shell #7 14" torte plate with silver sea horse decoration
2. Sea Shell #16 7" footed comport with "Charleton" decoration (view of top)
3. Sea Shell #7 14" torte plate with "Charleton" decoration

ROW 3
1. Sea Shell #2 7" plate with silver sea horse decoration - signed
2. Sea Shell #8 11" salad bowl with silver sea horse decoration
3. Sea Shell #2 7" plate

PLATE 37

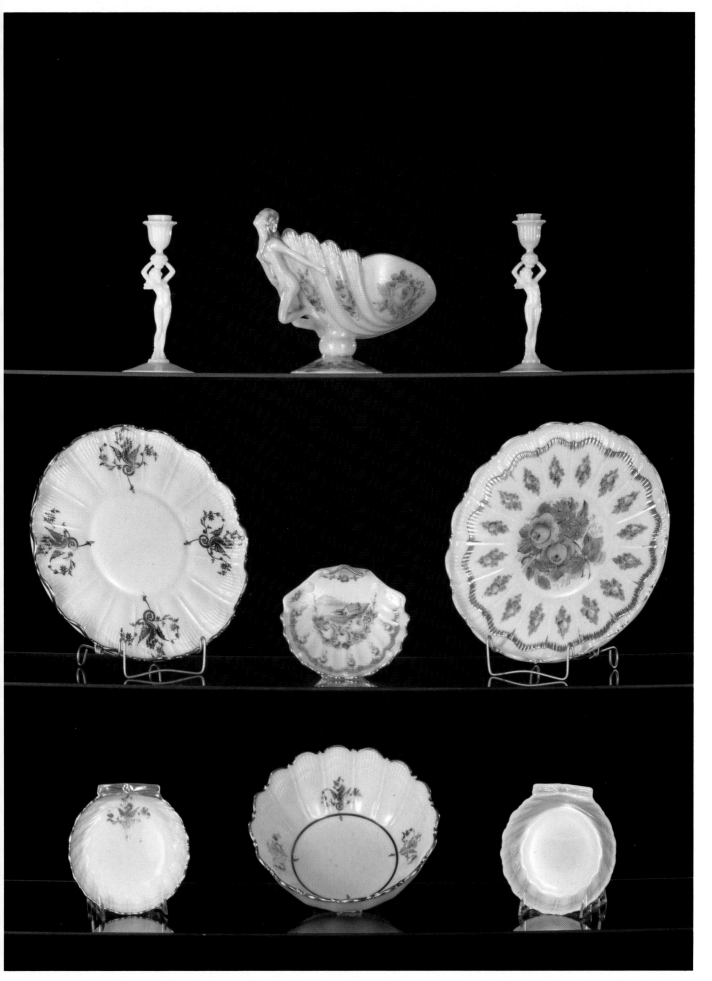

MOONLIGHT

Moonlight was introduced by June, 1936, and was used extensively until it was discontinued shortly after September, 1950. It was reintroduced in late 1955 or early 1956.

Moonlight is a light transparent blue that is slightly deeper in color than Willow (Eleanor) Blue. Moonlight tends to collect in the heavier portions of the glass and, in patterns such as Caprice, this will cause the color to appear darker or lighter depending upon the thickness of the pattern area being viewed.

ROW 1
1.   Caprice #202 cracker or pretzel jar
2.   Caprice #188 2 ounce tumbler
3.   Caprice #69 7½" 2-lite candlestick with seashell candle cups
4.   Caprice #252 blown 4½" vase
5.   #1222 turkey

ROW 2
1.   #1528 vase, engraved Starlite
2.   Bubble paperweight - faceted**
3.   #645 epergne - #1438 arm and #19 bobeche are Moonlight; vases, prisms and #1636 bird figure are Crystal
4.   Georgian #319/B/2 basket**
5.   #1321 decanter, crackle

ROW 3 (all items are Caprice)
1.   #200 goblet
2.   #100 5 ounce oil
3.   #344 3¼" globe vase
4.   #76 3-lite epergne - all Moonlight except prisms
5.   #91 salt and pepper
6.   #95 2" 4-footed almond
7.   #94 2½" 2-compartment individual nut and mint
8.   #167 6" covered candy

ROW 4 (all items are Caprice)
1,5 #1338 6" 3-lite candlesticks with silver decoration
2.   #13 3½" coaster
3.   11" bowl
4.   #93 2½" individual nut dish

**These items were introduced during the reopened period.

PLATE 38

WINDSOR BLUE

Windsor Blue, introduced in July, 1937, is a tone of icy blue in opaque glass used predominately in the Sea Shell Line. A few exceptions have been found in other lines, such as the Tally-Ho shaker shown in row 3. Extensive research has yielded no additional information on this color.

ROW 1
1. Sea Shell #16 7" comport - signed
2. Sea Shell #46 7½" flower holder
3. Sea Shell #15 6" cupped comport - signed

ROW 2
1. Slipper with kitten (John Degenhart mold)
2,4 Sea Shell #60 9" candlesticks - 1 with paper label
3. Sea Shell #14 9" comport - signed
5. Slipper with bow (John Degenhart mold)

ROW 3
1,4 #3400/647 6" candlestick
2. Sea Shell #47 9½" cornucopia
3. Tally-Ho #1402/51 handled cocktail shaker with #5 top

ROW 4
1. Daisy and Button hat (John Degenhart mold)
2. Sea Shell ash tray/card holder/cigarette snuffer - NOTE: will also take a small candle
3-7 Sea Shell #38 3½" x 2½" cigarette box with paper label and four Sea Shell #32 2¾" ash tray/card holders
8. Pair Sea Shell candleholders

Note: John Degenhart was an employee of Cambridge Glass for almost forty years. Prior to opening his own factory in 1947, he had a special arrangement with the Cambridge Glass Company to produce his own items. These items were produced from Cambridge glass using his molds and working on his own time.

PLATE 39

LaROSA

The earliest reference found for LaRosa is in a Cambridge Circular Letter dated March 25, 1938, regarding the availability of the Gyro Optic pattern. This is one of the colors discontinued October 16, 1943, due to material shortages brought about by World War II.

LaRosa is a medium to light pink color that shows gathering tendencies. In thick areas of the item the color is very strong, while in the thin areas it is very weak and transparent. There is a suggestion of orange tone when viewing into the edge of the blank.

The most predominate usage of this color was in the Caprice line, but it was also used in the Gyro Optic line, novelty baskets and "Varitone" sets.

ROW 1
1.   Caprice #300 9 ounce table goblet
2,4 Caprice #67 2½" candlesticks
3.   Caprice #82 13½" 4-footed salad bowl
5.   #496 12 ounce tall Joe

ROW 2 (entire row is Caprice pattern)
1.   #22 8½" salad plate
2.   #17 cup and saucer
3.   #165 6" covered candy
4.   #187 35 ounce decanter

ROW 3
1.   #1327 1 ounce cordial/favor vase
2.   Stradivari/Regency cordial
3.   Pristine #721 2½" square ash tray
4.   Caprice #300 12 ounce footed tumbler
5.   Sea Shell #34 3" 3-footed ash tray - Alpine
6.   Caprice #144 4" 2-handled jelly - Alpine
7.   Caprice #188 2 ounce tumbler - Alpine

Note: "Alpine" is a satin finish treatment on Caprice which is applied to a portion of the pattern. Alpine can be found on most Caprice colors and Crystal.

PLATE 40

PISTACHIO

Pistachio, like LaRosa, was introduced March 25, 1938, and was discontinued October 16, 1943, due to the scarcity of ingredients. The name Pistachio was used again during the reopened period (1955-58) but the colors differ.

It is the lightest shade of all the Cambridge greens. Although lighter in tone than light Emerald, it has more of a gathering property. It will appear to have more color in the thick areas of the blank than in thin areas.

It is a color with much sparkle and shows to advantage in a pattern such as Caprice. Pistachio was one of the colors often used in Varitone sets (see plate 56).

ROW 1
1.   #496 1 ounce little Joe
2.   Caprice #38 cream and sugar
3.   Martha #250 individual cream and sugar
4.   #1327 1 ounce cordial/favor vase

ROW 2
1.   #496 12 ounce tall Joe
2.   Georgian #319 9 ounce tumbler
3.   Stradivari/Regency cordial
4.   Stradivari/Regency cocktail
5.   #1371 Bridge Hound/dog cigarette holder
6.   Statuesque #3011 table goblet, crackle (this item is from the reopened period)
7.   Caprice #22 8½" salad plate - paper label
8.   Caprice #17 cup and saucer

ROW 3
1.   Gyro Optic #3143 10 ounce goblet
2.   Gyro Optic #3143 7 ounce sherbet
3.   Caprice #214 3" ash tray
4.   #321 9 ounce old-fashioned cocktail
5.   Sea Shell #34 3" 3-footed ash tray
6.   #1506/3 4½" novelty basket - signed
7.   Pristine #721 2½" square ash tray
8.   #1506/4 5" novelty basket (plate shaped) - signed

PLATE 41

MOCHA

Mocha, like LaRosa and Pistachio, was introduced March 25, 1938, and was discontinued October 16, 1943.

It is a soft shade of amber that is lighter than the Amber of the late 1920s. Due to the bunching or gathering effect, thicker areas of the blanks will appear to be much deeper in color. This color is easily confused with Madeira.

This color was used with the Caprice and Gyro Optic patterns and was one of the colors used in the Varitone and Harlequin sets.

ROW 1
1.   #321 9 ounce old-fashioned cocktail
2.   Caprice #300 9 ounce goblet
3.   Sea Shell #34 3″ 3-footed ash tray
4.   #518 8½″ figure flower holder (color is Madeira, see plate 15)
5.   #1371 Bridge Hound
6.   #496 12 ounce tall Joe
7.   #496 1 ounce little Joe

ROW 2 (entire row is Caprice pattern)
1.   #41 cream and sugar
2.   #300 6 ounce low sherbet
3.   #300 6 ounce tall sherbet
4.   #22 8½″ salad plate
5.   #17 cup and saucer

ROW 3
1.   Caprice #184 12 ounce tumbler
2.   Caprice #188 2 ounce tumbler
3.   #1506/4 5″ novelty basket (plate shaped) - signed
4.   #1327 1 ounce cordial/favor vase
5.   Stradivari/Regency cordial
6.   Stradivari/Regency cocktail

PLATE 42

MANDARIN GOLD

Mandarin Gold, introduced in August, 1949, was used until the factory closed in 1958.

A medium shade of yellow with considerable bunching in heavy areas of blanks, Mandarin Gold was a replacement for the lighter Gold Krystol.

ROW 1
1,3 Caprice #1338 3-lite candlesticks
2.   Caprice #66 4-footed 13″ oval bowl, crimped

ROW 2
1.   Cascade #4000/129 mayonnaise and underplate with Crystal ladle - mayonnaise has foil label
2.   #1311 4″ footed ash tray
3.   #1636 bird figure in Crystal Pristine #510 ball candlestick
4.   Bubble paperweight - faceted
5.   Cascade #4000/39 3-piece cream and sugar on tray

ROW 3
1.   #1715 ash tray/candleholder (shown candleholder side up)
2.   Pristine #734 4½″ round ash tray
3.   Caprice #133 6″ low footed bonbon, square
4.   #1956/5 8″ ash tray, ham bone
5.   #1715 ash tray/candleholder (shown ash tray side up)

PLATE 43

EMERALD

Introduced in August, 1949, Emerald was used until the demise of the Company in 1958. Cambridge collectors generally call this color late dark Emerald to differentiate it from the early dark Emerald of 1916 and the light Emerald of the 1920s and 1930s.

Emerald is often confused with the Forest Green color of earlier production. These two colors were not produced concurrently.

ROW 1
1. Covered candy (pattern name possibly Moderne)
2. Cascade #4000/39 3-piece cream and sugar on tray
3. Cascade #4000/165 covered candy
4. Caprice #151 5″ 2-handled jelly

ROW 2
1. Cascade #4000/573 9½″ vase
2. Pristine #510 Crystal ball candlestick with #1538 peg nappy candleholder and #1636 bird figure
3. #1713 4-piece smoker set
4. Georgian #316 sundae (see note below)
5. #3400/38 80 ounce ball shaped jug, optic

ROW 3
1. Sea Shell #35 cigarette box with enamel and gold decoration
2,4 Statuesque #3011/61 9″ candlesticks with Emerald candle cups and bobeches (see note below)
3. Sea Shell #40 10½″ flower or fruit center flying lady bowl (see note below)
5. Sea Shell #31 8″ 4-footed oval dish

ROW 4
1. Georgian #317 5 ounce tumbler
2,4 Pristine #499 Calla Lily candlesticks
3. Pristine #384 11″ oval bowl
5. #1536 peg nappy

Note: No evidence has been found to indicate that the #316 Georgian sundae, the Sea Shell #40 bowl or the #3011/61 candlesticks were produced in Emerald. Although these pieces appear to be a good color match, they may be Forest Green.

PLATE 44

MILK

Milk was introduced in January or February, 1954, and was apparently produced only until the initial closing of the factory in July, 1954. No mention of the color was found in advertisements or price lists of the reopened period 1955-58.

Milk is a white opaque color with no opalescence and a somewhat lifeless color which achieves it's beauty from the high shine that it provides.

ROW 1
1. W54 32 ounce jug
2. Pair W110 9″ Dolphin candlesticks, flat bottom, made for bobeche and prisms
3. W118 deviled egg plate

ROW 2
1. W105 9″ 3-footed bowl
2. W112 Sea Shell cream and sugar
3. W120 Dresden figure

ROW 3 (all with Charleton decoration)
1. W114 Sea Shell 7″ salad plate
2. W107 6″ footed candy box and cover
3. W101 cigarette box
4. W108 Sea Shell 8″ oval dish

ROW 4
1. W124 Caprice 4½″ vase
2. W63 individual cream and sugar - foil label
3. W94 3″ swan with gold decoration
4. #3400/156 12 ounce ball shaped decanter with stopper in brass Farber holder
5. W123 3″ urn
6. W74 Mount Vernon 5 ounce juice - foil label
7. W83 Mount Vernon salt and pepper

PLATE 45

EBON

Introduced in January or February, 1954, Ebon was apparently dropped with the initial factory closing in July of 1954.

To quote Cambridge: ''Ebon is a black glass with . . . a rough matte finish to which has been added a luster . . . which gives it a soft beauty . . . Ebon is both a treat and a treatment.'' It has a feel of velvet that is unique in glass manufacturing.

ROW 1 (all Cambridge Square pattern)
1.   #3797/91 5½" belled vase D/Birds
2.   #3797/78 9½" footed vase D/Stars
3.   #3797/91 5½" belled vase

ROW 2 (all Cambridge Square pattern)
1.   #3797/40 cigarette urn D/Stars - foil label
2.   #3797/80 8" footed bud vase D/Birds
3,5 #3797/493 1¾" block candlesticks D/Birds
4.   #3797/81 10" shallow bowl D/Birds
6.   #3797/80 8" footed bud vase
7.   #3797/40 cigarette urn D/Stars

ROW 3 (all Cambridge Square pattern)
1,5 #3797/493 1¾" block candlesticks D/Stars
2,4 #3797/69 oval 2-lite candlesticks D/Stars
3.   #3797/48 9" oval dish D/Birds

ROW 4 (all Cambridge Square pattern except #3 & #4)
1.   #3797/165 candy box and cover
2.   #3797/150 6½" ash tray
3.   Pristine #737 canoe ash tray D/Birds
4.   #1633 5" peg vase
5.   #3797/151 3½" ash tray D/Birds
6.   #3797/67 4½" candlestick D/Stars
7.   #3797/165 candy box and cover D/Stars

PLATE 46

SMOKE

Smoke was introduced after the March 15, 1955, reopening of the plant and was one of the colors listed in the March 15, 1956, Price List. The specific date of introduction is not known, only that it occurred during the one year period mentioned above.

Smoke is a medium shade of transparent gray. Many of the pieces produced in this color will show a strong suggestion of amethyst.

ROW 1
1.   Jefferson #1401 12 ounce footed ice tea
2.   Jefferson #1401 10 ounce goblet
3.   Jefferson #1401 6 ounce tall sherbet
4,6 Candlesticks **
5.   Candy without cover **

ROW 2
1.   #1528 vase D/Stars - foil label
2.   Allegro #3795 wine, crackle **
3.   Allegro #3795 cordial, crackle **
4.   #577 8″ Horn of Plenty
5.   Statuesque #3011/25 4½″ ivy ball, 9½″ tall
6.   #1040 3″ swan
7.   #1529 decanter, engraved Wedding Rings

ROW 3
1.   Georgian #319 12 ounce tumbler - foil label
2.   Georgian #319/B/2 basket **
3.   #1371 Bridge Hound
4.   Georgian #317 5 ounce tumbler
5.   Georgian #319/S sherbet

ROW 4
1.   #1956/1 10″ ash tray **
2.   #1956/2 10″ ash tray with peg **
3.   #1957/6 ash tray **

** These items were introduced during the reopened period.

PLATE 47

MARDI GRAS

Mardi Gras, introduced in December, 1957, incorporated swirls and flecks of vivid colors into a Crystal bodied ware in an unusual line of shapes.

The White Rain and Blue Cloud items shown in this plate were introduced a little earlier than Mardi Gras as they were listed in the October 1, 1956 Price List. Since they are similar in composition, they are generally considered by collectors to be part of the Mardi Gras line.

White Rain is flecks of a light pink opaque (possibly Crown Tuscan), and Blue Cloud is flecks of a light blue opaque (possibly Windsor Blue). The items shown with the orange flecks were probably called "Strawberry."

ROW 1
1.   Casual line #3060 sherbet - "Strawberry"
2.   Casual line #3060 sherbet - Blue Cloud
3.   Casual line #3060 sherbet - Blue Cloud
4.   Casual line #3060 sherbet - White Rain

ROW 2
1.   12" vase
2.   Sea Shell #33 4" ash tray (see note below)
3.   17½" vase - foil label
4.   4½" vase
5.   12" vase

ROW 3
1.   Small bowl - foil label
2.   Sea Shell #46 7½" shell flower holder (see note below)
3.   Ball vase

Note: These items are Mardi Gras style, but are not listed among the twenty items in the Mardi Gras line.

PLATE 48

VIOLET, AMBER, SUNSET, PINK, PISTACHIO

All of the colors on this plate are unique to the reopened period March, 1955, through 1958. Several new shapes were introduced during this period. They are the key to identifying these colors.

Violet is a medium shade of opaque purple, lighter than Helio of the 1920s. It will not be found in the same shapes as Helio.

Amber is a name long used by the Company, but after the factory reopening a formula change produced a considerably darker color. Collectors call this color late Amber to differentiate it from the earlier ambers.

Sunset, a multicolor presentation, is a beautiful dark red at the bottom of the item shading through yellow and sometimes green into a light transparent blue, topped off by a thin line of yellow and red at the top. Sunset is very similar to the Rubina color of the 1920s.

"Pink" is a light transparent color. This is not a unique color. It can only be positively identified in shapes introduced during the reopened period.

Pistachio is a light transparent green with less sparkle than the earlier color of this name. Under black light the late formula does not produce the glow apparent in each of the other light greens.

ROW 1 (all items are Violet)
1. Jenny Lind #315 covered candy **
2. Sea Shell #33 4" 3-footed ash tray
3. Caprice #66 12" oval bowl
4. Mount Vernon #2 6½ ounce tall sherbet
5. Everglade #20 10½" vase

ROW 2 (all items are Violet)
1. Everglade #23 5" globe vase
2. Arcadia #39 12½" oval bowl
3. Arcadia #165 covered candy
4. #1956/5 8" ash tray **
5. Everglade #22 6" vase

ROW 3
1. Amber Jenny Lind #317 5" rose bowl **
2. Amber Georgian #319/B/3 basket **
3. Sunset #1955 3 ounce tumbler **
4. Sunset #1955 6 ounce tumbler **
5. Sunset #1955 14 ounce tumbler **
6. Sunset #1955 14 ounce tumbler - foil label **

ROW 4
1. "Pink" #1528 10½" vase, crackle - foil label
2. "Pink" #1955 14 ounce tumbler, crackle **
3. "Pink" #1955 3 ounce tumbler, crackle **
4. Pistachio #1528 10½" vase, engraved Wedding Rings
5. Pistachio Statuesque #3011 table goblet, crackle
6. Pistachio #1956/5 8" ash tray **

** These items were introduced during the reopened period.

PLATE 49

EXPERIMENTAL COLORS

There is no evidence that any of the colors shown on this plate were regular production colors or had names applied to them.

ROW 1
1. #3400/68 cream and sugar - both signed
2. Decagon #815 7½″ plate - signed
3. #1309 5″ vase
4. #3400/68 cream - signed

ROW 2
1. #3400/68 sugar - signed
2. Sea Shell #1 5″ bread and butter plate
3. Sea Shell #8 11″ salad bowl
4. Sea Shell #1 5″ bread and butter plate
5. #3400/68 cream

ROW 3
1. Sea Shell #1 5″ bread and butter plate
2. Sea Shell #18 10″ 3-footed bowl - signed
3. #3400/68 cream - signed

ROW 4
1. Everglade #2 5″ 1-lite candlestick
2. Everglade #10 3½″ l-lite candlestick
3. Sea Shell #4 5″ bread and butter plate
4. Stratford #102 oval 2-handled salt dip
5. Everglade #42 7″ crimped comport

PLATE 50

COMPARISON OF OPAQUE COLORS

In the following plates an attempt has been made to give the reader an opportunity to compare some of the subtle differences found in colors, especially some of the colors that are often confused. This is an unusual opportunity to present two or more distinct colors, identifiable by vintage of the shape or decoration, in close proximity under identical lighting conditions.

ROW 1
Avocado
   1.   Bookend
   2.   Candlestick
   3.   Plainware #1917/20 sugar
Jade
   4.   Twist candlestick
   5.   Special Article #96 ½ pound candy jar
   6.   Special Article #63 6″ comport

ROW 2
Primrose
   1.   Candlestick/Vase
   2.   Special Article #14 10″ bowl
   3.   Candlestick
Ivory
   4.   #509 8½″ two-kid flower holder
   5.   #174 9 ounce syrup pitcher with metal top
   6.   Large bitters bottle

ROW 3
Helio
   1.   Special Article #94 sweet pea vase with platinum edge
   2.   Perfume atomizer with gold and black enamel trim
   3.   Top hat cigarette holder
   4.   Special Article #90 8″ stick vase
Violet
   5.   Arcadia #39 12½″ oval bowl
   6.   Jenny Lind #315 covered candy

ROW 4
Azurite
   1.   #133 3″ x 5″ cigarette box
   2.   Community #2800/237 16 ounce night bottle, tumbler missing
   3.   Special Article #6 6¼″ bowl
Windsor Blue
   4.   Sea Shell #14 9″ comport - signed
   5.   Sea Shell candleholder
   6.   #647 6″ candlestick

PLATE 51

COMPARISON OF TRANSPARENT GREEN COLORS

The first two rows in this color plate show the light greens - Emerald from the late 1920s and early 1930s, Pistachio items from the late 1930s and early 1940s. The Topaz piece is shown here to emphasis that it is distinctly yellow when compared to the green family.

ROW 1
Light Emerald
1. Weatherford sugar
2. Georgian #319 9 ounce tumbler
3. #1191 Cherub candleholder
4. #170 9 ounce syrup with metal cover

ROW 2
Topaz
1. Chelsea #4070/144 ½ pound covered candy
Pistachio
2. Georgian #319 9 ounce tumbler
3. Caprice #38 sugar
4. Caprice #17 cup

Row 3 shows examples of early dark Emerald from the Near Cut era. In row 4, late dark Emerald is represented by pieces from the late 1940s and the 1950s, while Forest Green is represented by pieces from the 1930s. Some items in these last two colors are extremely difficult to distinguish under most lighting conditions. Forest Green items *generally* show a yellowish cast while late Emerald items *generally* do not. Since both colors are found in a range of shading, no clear-cut rule can be stated to differentiate these colors. Most collectors rely heavily on knowledge of the production period of the shapes.

ROW 3
Early dark Emerald
1. #2766 Thistle pitcher with gold encrusting - signed NEAR CUT
2. #2840 7" vase with crimped top
3. #2766 Thistle cream with gold encrusting - signed NEAR CUT

ROW 4
Emerald
1. Covered candy
2. Pristine #499 Calla Lily candlestick
3. Cascade #4000/165 covered candy
Forest Green
4. Mount Vernon #84 14 ounce stein
5. #3400/46 12 ounce cabinet flask
6. Everglade #26 cream

PLATE 52

COMPARISON OF TRANSPARENT BLUE COLORS

Moonlight blue is identifiable by the Caprice shape in the first two items and by the late period (1955-1958) bubble paperweight. On the right, the Willow Blue is identifiable by the Everglade and Decagon shapes from the 1920s and early 1930s. The Willow Blue items are more evenly colored and slightly lighter than the Moonlight blue items.

ROW 1
Moonlight blue
1.   Caprice #167 6″ covered candy
2.   Caprice #200 goblet
3.   Bubble paperweight - faceted
Willow Blue
4.   Pair Everglade #10 3½″ candlesticks
5.   Decagon #1095 3-piece sugar and cream set

Row 2 shows examples of the medium to dark blues of the 1920s. These blues become progressively darker through the sequence of Cobalt Blue 1, Cobalt Blue 2 and Ritz Blue. Notice the greener cast of Bluebell compared to the cobalts.

ROW 2
Bluebell
1.   #518 8½″ figure flower holder
Ritz Blue
2.   Plainware #1917/88 1 pound candy jar, optic, with grey cutting
Cobalt Blue 2
3.   9″ candlestick
Cobalt Blue 1
4.   Plainware #1917/88 ½ pound candy jar, optic

Row 3 illustrates the very dark Royal Blues. These colors rarely cause confusion because of the significantly different time frame. Any Near Cut era shape means that it is the early Royal Blue, while all others are the Royal Blue introduced in 1931.

ROW 3
Royal Blue
1,2   Gadroon #3500/42 12″ urn and cover
3.   Gadroon #3500/74 4″ candlestick with ram's heads
Early Royal Blue
4.   Colonial #2630 4-piece toy tea set

PLATE 53

COMPARISON OF PINK COLORS

Representative pieces in row 1 illustrate the broad color range that can be found in Crown Tuscan.

ROW 1
Crown Tuscan
1. #1283 8″ vase with Ebony foot
2. #1337 cigarette cup with Ebony ash tray foot
3. #3400/114 64 ounce ball shaped jug
4. #7966 2 ounce sherry
5. #1321 28 ounce decanter

With good examples of Crown Tuscan and Coral, row 2 shows no discernible difference between the colors. The characteristic bluish opalescence in the thinner areas of the Sea Shell shapes can be seen better on plate 37.

ROW 2
Crown Tuscan
1. Cascade #4000/671 ice bucket
2. Nautilus #3450 28 ounce decanter
Coral
3. #702 miniature cornucopia
4. Sea Shell #2 7″ plate
5. Sea Shell #61 9″ candlestick made for bobeche and prisms (also #3011 Statuesque line)

Row 3 shows the variation in the shades of Peach-blo. All of the shapes shown were introduced during the mid to late 1920s.

ROW 3
Peach-blo
1. #518 8½″ figure flower holder
2. #2746 cigar or tobacco jar
3. Georgian #319 9 ounce tumbler
4. #647 6″ 2-lite candlestick, plate etched Diane
5. Aero Optic #8701 tumbler

Row 4 shows items in the extremely similar colors, Peach-blo and LaRosa. LaRosa will rarely be found in items other than the Caprice and #3143 Gyro Optic lines. A slight orange cast may be seen in the LaRosa items.

ROW 4
Peach-blo
1. #3400/130 11 ounce tumbler
2. #1196 bathroom bottle, acid etched "Cotton"
LaRosa
3. Caprice #165 6″ covered candy
4. Caprice #187 35 ounce jug

PLATE 54

MORE TRANSPARENT COLOR COMPARISONS

Mulberry is identifiable by the powder jar and the covered candy from the mid-1920s and Amethyst by the shapes introduced during the 1930s and 1940s. Note that the Mulberry items are distinctively lighter than the Amethyst pieces.

ROW 1
Mulberry
1. Square knobbed powder box
2. Honeycomb 8″ covered candy
3. Georgian #319 9 ounce tumbler
Amethyst
4. #1330 5″ Sweet Potato vase
5. #1369 36 ounce Melon fluted decanter
6. Tally-Ho #1402/44 15 ounce tumbler

The Topaz items in the second row are identified with the early to mid-1920s by the Stratford jug which bears the large triangle C mark. Note the green cast of Topaz compared to Gold Krystol and Mandarin Gold items in row 3.

ROW 2
Topaz
1. Stratford #5 2 pint handled jug
2. 8 ounce dog bottle with tumbler cap
3. Georgian #319 9 ounce tumbler

Gold Krystol and Mandarin Gold are frequently confused colors. From this comparison the darker appearance of Mandarin Gold should be evident.

ROW 3
Gold Krystol
1. #3400/9 7″ candy box and cover, plate etched Apple Blossom
2. Mount Vernon #84 14 ounce stein
3. #646 5″ candlestick
Mandarin Gold
4. Cascade #4000/129 mayonnaise bowl
5. #1956/5 8″ ash tray
6. Caprice #1338 3-lite candlestick

The 1955-1958 Amber shown in the Jenny Lind rose bowl is darker than the earlier ambers. Mocha, like its contemporary color LaRosa, has a slight orange cast. Madeira is very similar to Mocha and can be differentiated best by the production period of the shape.

ROW 4
1. Amber 9″ footed bowl with ram's head handles
2. Amber Dolphin candlestick
3. Late Amber Jenny Lind #317 rose bowl
4. Mocha Caprice #17 cup
5. Mocha Caprice #184 12 ounce tumbler
6. Madeira #518 8½″ figure flower holder

PLATE 55

HARLEQUIN AND VARITONE SETS

First shown on a June, 1941, catalog page, Harlequin sets consist of eight pieces of the same shape in eight different colors. Since some colors were dropped and others were added, more than eight colors can be found in Harlequin items.

Varitone sets were introduced about the same time as Harlequin sets. These sets consisted of a varying number of pieces depending on the set, but with four light transparent colors. Due to the color availability, the colors used may vary from set to set. Cambridge also made Rainbow sets with four dark transparent colors. No Rainbow sets are illustrated.

ROW 1
#1327 1 ounce cordial/favor vases
   1.   LaRosa
   2.   Ebony
   3.   Tahoe blue
   4.   Mocha
   5.   Forest Green
   6.   Gold Krystol
   7.   unknown green
   8.   Pistachio
   9.   Amethyst
   10. Moonlight blue
#496 1 ounce little Joes
   11. Pistachio
   12. Mocha

ROW 2
Stradivari/Regency cordials
   1.   Pistachio
   2.   Gold Krystol
   3.   Mocha
   4.   Moonlight blue
   5.   LaRosa
Stradivari/Regency cocktails
   6.   Mocha
   7.   Moonlight blue
   8.   Forest Green
   9.   Amethyst
   10. Tahoe blue
   11. Gold Krystol
   12. Pistachio

ROW 3
#728 5-piece ash tray set, Crystal holder (not Varitone due to the Amber item)
   1.   Moonlight blue
   2.   Amber
   3.   Gold Krystol
   4.   Crystal
#496 12 ounce tall Joes
   5.   Forest Green
   6.   Mocha
   7.   Amethyst
   8.   Pistachio
   9.   Moonlight blue
   10. Gold Krystol
   11. LaRosa
   12. Tahoe blue

ROW 4
#321 7 ounce old-fashioned cocktails
   1.   Pistachio
   2.   Tahoe blue
   3.   Moonlight blue
   4.   Forest Green
   5.   Mocha
   6.   Amethyst
#728 5-piece ash tray set, Crystal holder - Varitone
   7.   Gold Krystol
   8.   Moonlight blue
   9.   Pistachio
   10. LaRosa

PLATE 56

3011 STATUESQUE LINE

The Statuesque line is very popular among collectors due to the variety of shapes and colors. The #9 3 ounce cocktails and the #13 1 ounce brandies were sold as Harlequin sets (see plate 56).

ROW 1
1. Amber #29 4″ mint dish
2. Amethyst comport insert in Farber holder
3. Topaz hoch bowl on 6″ stem
4. Heatherbloom #1 banquet goblet, optic
5. Amethyst #26 bud vase
6. Crown Tuscan 7″ flared comport, #3400 line pattern in top
7. Royal Blue ash tray

ROW 2
1. Carmen covered sweetmeat
2,4 Pair candlesticks with bobeches and prisms - candle cup and bobeches are Emerald (possibly Forest Green)
3. Emerald #11 7″ cupped comport
5. Carmen #25 ivy ball

ROW 3 (all items are #9 3 ounce cocktails)
1. Amethyst, unfinished
2. Mandarin Gold
3. Amethyst bowl on Crown Tuscan stem
4. Ebony bowl and foot - Crystal stem
5. Tahoe blue
6. Smoke, crackle
7. Carmen, crackle, on 5″ stem

ROW 4
1. Amethyst #14 1 ounce cordial
2. Amber #13 1 ounce brandy on frosted stem
3. Forest Green #6 5 ounce roemer
4. ''Pink'' #3 saucer champagne
5. Royal Blue #7 4½ ounce claret
6. Pistachio #2 crackle table goblet
7. Amethyst #1 banquet goblet
8. Windsor Blue 9″ candlestick

PLATE 57

FLOWER HOLDERS

Flower holders, commonly called flower frogs, are another popular category among collectors due to the variety of shapes and colors.

ROW 1
1. Crown Tuscan #70 turtle
2. Peach-blo #2899 2¼", marked "PAT D APRIL 11 1916"
3. Gold Krystol #2899 3" with patent date
4. Crown Tuscan #2899 3"
5. Amber #2899 4" with patent date
6. Moonlight blue #1502 4" insert for Caprice rose bowl - marked "Patent Applied for"
7. Light Emerald #2899 4" with patent date

ROW 2
1. Moonlight blue #1137 5¼" Blue Jay
2. Crown Tuscan #518 8½" draped lady
3. Light Emerald #849 8½" draped lady, oval base
4. Amber #518 8½" draped lady
5. Peach-blo #514 5½" eagle

ROW 3
1. Moonlight blue #1114 6½" bashful charlotte, frosted
2. Peach-blo 8¾" two-kid, oval base - paper label
3. Moonlight blue #509 two-kid, round base
4. Ivory #512 9½" rose lady on early scalloped base
5. Amber #512 8½" rose lady on round base
6. Light Emerald #1108 9" mandolin lady, frosted

ROW 4
1. Peach-blo #522 11" two bun Oriental figure on base with metal retaining ring (very dark shade)
2. Ivory #513 13" draped lady on early scalloped base
3. Peach-blo melon boy
4. Amber #513 13" draped lady
5. Light Emerald #523 one bun Oriental figure (Geisha) on base with metal retaining ring

PLATE 58

SMALL ITEMS

This plate shows a variety of shapes and colors that can be collected in small pieces. Cambridge has provided an abundance of such items for the collector with limited space.

ROW 1

1. Avocado pin holder
2. Windsor Blue Sea Shell ash tray/card holder/cigarette snuffer
3. Milk #W123 3″ urn
4. Coral #702 miniature cornucopia
5. Crown Tuscan Nautilus #3450 2 ounce tumbler
6. Ebon Cambridge Square #3797/40 cigarette urn D/Stars
7. Ebony #1626 cigarette lighter

ROW 2

1. Ivory perfume atomizer with black enamel and gold bands
2. Carrara #2800/235 pin tray - signed
3. Azurite #2795 3″ toilet box
4. Jade mayonnaise ladle
5. Primrose ring tree
6. Helio small basket
7. Violet Sea Shell #33 4″ ash tray

ROW 3

1. Light Emerald door knob
2. 1903 Amber top hat cigarette holder
3. Forest Green Nautilus #3450 1½ ounce decanter
4. Rubina wide optic cocktail
5. Mandarin Gold bubble paperweight
6. LaRosa Caprice #188 2 ounce tumbler with Alpine
7. Amethyst Caprice #188 2 ounce tumbler
8. Carmen Nautilus #3450 2½ ounce tumbler
9. Royal Blue #1217 4 ounce bitters bottle
10. Emerald #1712 3½″ ash tray

ROW 4

1. Moonlight blue Caprice #212 3½ coaster
2. Sunset #1955 3 ounce tumbler
3. Green Carnival #2675 2 ounce perfume
4. Mulberry night tumbler
5. Amethyst Star #1 2½″ candlestick
6. Topaz perfume
7. Heatherbloom #1203 1 ounce shammed shot glass
8. Smoke Allegro #3795 cordial, crackle
9. Bluebell ink bottle - stopper missing
10. Cobalt Blue 2 #1 Keg set tumbler

ROW 5

#1371 Bridge Hounds

1. Mocha	3. Amber	5. Tahoe blue	Frogs 7. Light Emerald, frosted
2. Gold Krystol	4. Crown Tuscan	6. Smoke	8. Light Emerald

#1371 Bridge Hounds

			#1style Moths (in front of Bridge Hounds)
9. Milk	11. Ebony	13. Pistachio	15. Peach-blo, frosted
10. Amethyst	12. Late dark Emerald	14. Peach-blo	16. Peach-blo

ROW 6

Yardley Jars

1. Ivory with gold label "Yardley Lotus Sachet"
2. Pink, frosted
3. Light pink opaque "English Complexion Cream"
4. Dark pink opaque
5. Tan with glass lid

Prism signs

6. Royal Blue with gold encrusted lettering
7. Peach-blo
8. Light Emerald with gold encrusted lettering

Birds

9. Light Emerald #3 style
10. Light Emerald #2 style

ROW 7

1. Heatherbloom #3400/71 3″ nut cup - signed
2. Peach-blo #3400/71 3″ nut cup - paper label
3. Gold Krystol #3400/70 3½″ cranberry, plate etched Apple Blossom
4. Willow Blue #3400/70 3½″ cranberry - signed
5. Pistachio Sea Shell #34 3-footed ash tray
6. Marigold Carnival Sea Shell #34 3-footed ash tray
7. "Pink" #1955 3 ounce tumbler, crackle

PLATE 59

SWANS

Any book on Cambridge glass would be incomplete without a presentation on swans which are extremely popular among collectors. The #1221 16″ (punch bowl) and the #1045 13″ swans are not illustrated.

ROW 1
1. Crown Tuscan #1043 8½″, "Charleton" decoration
2. Crown Tuscan #1043 8½″, "Charleton" decoration

ROW 2
1. Ebony #1041 4½″ - signed
2. Milk #1041 4½″
3. Manadarin Gold #1042 6½″

ROW 3
1. Amber #1043 8½″
2. Peach-blo #1044 10″
3. Moonlight blue #1043 8½″ - signed

ROW 4
1. Smoke #1040 3″
2. Peach-blo #1040 3″
3. Gold Krystol #1040 3″
4. Carmen #1040 3″
5. Milk #1040 3″, gold trim

PLATE 60

Price Guide to

Colors in Cambridge Glass

INTRODUCTION

This publication is not a *price list*. It is a *price guide* for pieces shown in National Cambridge Collectors, Inc. *Colors in Cambridge Glass.* It does not establish prices, but suggests what the collector might expect to pay at this time. It does not project future prices. An increase in most prices can reasonably be expected due to the increasing number of collectors of this fine glassware.

This prices presented are the result of averaging prices provided by a relatively large group of knowledgeable Cambridge Glass collectors. Prices in some parts of the United States will vary from those shown due to regional demand and availability.

Prices are for single pieces, except where noted, in mint condition. Poor color, stains, worn decoration or damages will detract from the prices shown.

We remind you that this is a *price guide*. The price that you pay must be based upon your desires, circumstances, and the geographical area.

Those persons who desire more information and knowledge of Cambridge Glass are encouraged to seek membership in:

National Cambridge Collectors, Inc.
Dept PG 6
P.O. Box 416
Cambridge, Ohio 43725

*Not Cambridge

PLATE 1
Row 1
1. $24.00
2. $26.00
3. $23.00
Row 2
1. $137.00
2. $48.00
3. $34.00
4. $33.00
5. $40.00
6. $30.00
Row 3
1. $135.00
2. $28.00
3. $37.00

Row 3
1. $55.00
2. $100.00
3. $220.00
4. $800.00
5. $75.00
6. $100.00
7. $65.00
8. $155.00
Row 4
1. $150.00
2. $625.00
3. $140.00
4. $175.00
5. $275.00
6. $185.00
7. $55.00

3. $45.00
4. $1,500.00
5. $95.00
6. $60.00
7. $65.00

PLATE 2
Row 1
1. $165.00
2. $350.00
3. $150.00
Row 2
1. $180.00
2. *
3. $75.00
4. $180.00
Row 3
1. $130.00
2. $140.00
3. $50.00
Row 4
1. $40.00
2. $50.00
3. $70.00
4. $22.00
5. $40.00

PLATE 3
Row 1
1. $225.00
2. $485.00
3. $275.00
Row 2
1. $340.00
2. $700.00
3. $175.00

PLATE 4
Row 1
1. $100.00
2. $105.00
3. $100.00
Row 2
1. $65.00
2. $22.00
3. $45.00
4. $75.00
5. $40.00
6. $80.00
7. $50.00
Row 3
1. $150.00
2. $175.00
3. $200.00
4. $80.00
5. $75.00
6. $40.00
7. $210.00
8. $70.00
9. $85.00
10. $60.00
11. $90.00
Row 4
1. $55.00
2. $165.00

PLATE 5
Row 1
1. $185.00
2. $190.00
3. $180.00
Row 2
1,5. $300.00
2. $165.00
3. $275.00
4. $280.00
Row 3
1. $45.00
2. $45.00
3. $120.00
4. $105.00
5. $65.00
6. $180.00
7. $40.00
8. $350.00
Row 4
1. $400.00
2. $22.00
3. $125.00
4. $65.00
5. $600.00
6. $22.00
7. $150.00
8. $45.00
9. $180.00

PLATE 6
Row 1
1. $185.00
2,4. $80.00
3. $50.00
5. $55.00
Row 2
1. $50.00
2. $45.00
3. $40.00
4. $75.00

5. $65.00
6. $80.00
Row 3
1. $75.00
2. $70.00
3. $315.00
4. $55.00
5. $140.00
6. $80.00
Row 4
1. $105.00
2. $180.00
3. $45.00
4. $350.00
5. $50.00

PLATE 7
Row 1
1. $27.00
2. $39.00
3. $45.00
4. $55.00
5. $40.00
Row 2
1. $40.00
2. $75.00
3,5. $80.00
4. $75.00
6. $185.00
7. $135.00
8. $58.00
Row 3
1. $75.00
2. $35.00
3. $135.00
4. $55.00
5. $55.00
6. $60.00
7. $60.00
Row 4
1. $85.00
2. $40.00
3. $350.00
4. $35.00

5. $70.00
PLATE 8
Row 1
1,3. $250.00
2. $320.00
Row 2
1,5. $130.00
2. $135.00
3. $55.00
4. $95.00
Row 3
1. $185.00
2. $175.00
3,5. $130.00
4. $190.00
6. $215.00
Row 4
1. $135.00
2. $65.00
3. $65.00
4. $45.00
5. $60.00
6. $40.00
7. $200.00
8. $45.00
9. $340.00

PLATE 9
Row 1
1,3. $80.00
2. $35.00
Row 2
1. $175.00
2. $100.00
3-5. $160.00†
6. $125.00
(† is price for 5-piece set)
Row 3
1. $145.00
2. $60.00
3. $275.00
4. $37.00
5. $300.00
Row 4
1. $55.00
2. $75.00

3. $70.00
4. $50.00
5. $80.00
6. $85.00
7. $60.00
PLATE 10
Row 1
1. $55.00
2. $50.00
Row 2
1. $80.00
2. $40.00
3. $175.00
Row 3
1. $25.00
2. $45.00
3. $130.00
4. $50.00
5. $45.00
Row 4
1. $48.00
2. $40.00

PLATE 11
Row 1
1,3. $175.00
2. $70.00
Row 2
1. $32.00
2. $120.00
3. $37.00
4. $33.00
5. $32.00
6. $28.00
7. $38.00
Row 3
1. $385.00
2. $250.00
3. $90.00
4. $250.00
5. $560.00
6. $300.00
Row 4
1,2. $65.00
3. $50.00
4. $60.00

5. $55.00
6. $75.00
7. $63.00
8. $65.00
9. $35.00
10. $50.00

PLATE 12
Row 1
1. $65.00
2. $35.00
3. $42.00
Row 2
1. $35.00
2. $47.00
3. $48.00
4. $32.00
5. $38.00
6. $38.00
7. $47.00
Row 3
1. $105.00
2-4. $400.00
5. $85.00
Row 4
1. $55.00
2. $155.00
3. $90.00
4. $100.00
5. $75.00
6. $50.00
7. $65.00

PLATE 13
Row 1
1. $80.00
2. $100.00
3. $65.00
4. $200.00
5. $85.00
Row 2
1. $48.00
2. $45.00
3. $710.00
4. $82.00
5. $122.00

Row 3
1. $180.00
2. $225.00
3. $185.00
4. $185.00
5. $200.00
Row 4
1. $95.00
2. $135.00
3. $345.00
4. $175.00
5. $350.00
PLATE 14
Row 1
1,3. $500.00
2. $70.00
Row 2
1. $1,000.00
2. $500.00
3. $1,250.00
Row 3
1. $90.00
2. $65.00
3. $70.00
4. $85.00
PLATE 15
Row 1
1. $150.00
2. $75.00
3. $300.00
4. $65.00
5. $65.00
Row 2
1. $45.00
2,3,5 $355.00
4. $95.00
6. $80.00
Row 3
1. $65.00
2. $65.00
3. $70.00
4. $60.00
5. $85.00
6. $95.00
Row 4
1. $55.00
2. $45.00
3. $55.00
4. $32.00
5. $20.00
6. $55.00
7. $58.00
8. $52.00
PLATE 16
Row 1
1. $85.00
2. $55.00
3. $185.00
Row 2
1. $48.00
2. $40.00
3. $55.00
4. $60.00
5. $35.00
Row 3
1. $425.00
2. $500.00
3. $375.00
Row 4
1. $68.00
2. $145.00
3. $27.00
4. $30.00
5. $24.00
6. $15.00
7. $25.00
PLATE 17
Row 1
1. $200.00

2. $385.00
3. $38.00
Row 2
1. $48.00
2. $60.00
3. $55.00
Row 3
1. $23.00
2. $150.00
3. $37.00
PLATE 18
Row 1
1. $225.00
2. $105.00
3. $535.00
4. $105.00
5. $180.00
Row 2
1,3. $500.00
2. $850.00
Row 3
1. $225.00
2. $100.00
3. $100.00
4. $100.00
5. $155.00
Row 4
1. $150.00
2. $140.00
3. $150.00
4. $420.00
PLATE 19
Row 1
1. $120.00
2. $220.00
3. $175.00
Row 2
1,3. $800.00
2. $125.00
Row 3
1. $135.00
2. $200.00
3. $125.00
4. $135.00
Row 4
1. $190.00
2. $175.00
3. $95.00
4. $125.00
PLATE 20
Row 1
1. $80.00
2. $85.00
3. $135.00
4. $55.00
Row 2
1. $40.00
2. $120.00
3. $65.00
4. $120.00
5. $48.00
Row 3
1. $375.00
2. $180.00
3. $40.00
4. $90.00
5. $85.00
6. $110.00
7. $25.00
8. $32.00
Row 4
1. $40.00
2. $40.00
3. $40.00
4. $22.00
5,6. $410.00
7. $62.00
8. $42.00

9. $50.00
PLATE 21
Row 1
1. $47.00
2. $55.00
3. $22.00
4. $105.00
5. $45.00
Row 2
1. $335.00
2. $48.00
3. $350.00
Row 3
1. $50.00
2. $55.00
3. $85.00
4. $80.00
5. $85.00
Row 4
1,3. $500.00
2. $500.00
PLATE 22
Row 1
1. $600.00
2. $375.00
3. $625.00
Row 2
1. $60.00
2,4. $110.00
3. $38.00
5. $75.00
Row 3
1. $85.00
2. $130.00
3. $60.00
4. $95.00
5. $100.00
6. $85.00
7. $725.00
8. $90.00
Row 4
1. $33.00
2. $100.00
3. $18.00
4. $45.00
5. $25.00
PLATE 23
Row 1
1,3. $90.00
2. $75.00
Row 2
1. $120.00
2. $60.00
3. $210.00
Row 3
1,2. $55.00
3. $65.00
4. $30.00
5. $20.00
6. $140.00
7. $50.00
Row 4
1,3. $275.00
2. $200.00
PLATE 24
Row 1
1,3. $65.00
2. $350.00
Row 2
1,3. $75.00
2. $150.00
Row 3
1. $135.00
2. $160.00
3. $50.00
PLATE 25
Row 1
1. $37.00

2,4. $65.00
3. $225.00
5. $140.00
Row 2
1. $40.00
2. $40.00
3. $42.00
4. $47.00
Row 3
1. $48.00
2. $95.00
3. $100.00
4. $60.00
Row 4
1. $40.00
2. $48.00
3. $75.00
4. $115.00
5. $60.00
PLATE 26
Row 1
1. $50.00
2. $330.00
3. $60.00
4. $75.00
Row 2
1,3. $120.00
2. $250.00
Row 3
1. $115.00
2. $80.00
3. $425.00
Row 4
1. $400.00
2. $28.00
3. $35.00
4. $50.00
5. $85.00
PLATE 27
Row 1
1,3. $800.00
2. $850.00
Row 2
1. $1,700.00
2. $1,325.00
3. $2,200.00
Row 3
1. $300.00
2. $100.00
3. $110.00
4. $110.00
5. $220.00
Row 4
1. $120.00
2. $125.00
3. $165.00
PLATE 28
Row 1
1. $145.00
2. $140.00
3. $280.00
Row 2
1. $80.00
2. $710.00
3. $90.00
Row 3
1. $275.00
2. $145.00
3. $115.00
4. $265.00
5. $80.00
6. $125.00
7. $390.00
Row 4
1. $160.00
2,4. $375.00
3. $375.00

5. $120.00
PLATE 29
Row 1
1. $115.00
2. $60.00
3. *
4. $95.00
Row 2
1. $300.00
2. $65.00
3. $300.00
4. $275.00
5. $40.00
6. $45.00
Row 3
1. $65.00
2. $24.00
3. $175.00
4. $135.00
5. $130.00
6. $60.00
7. $80.00
Row 4
1. $26.00
2. $42.00
3. $120.00
4,6. $130.00
5. $45.00
7. $180.00
PLATE 30
Row 1
1. $45.00
2. $50.00
3. $65.00
4. $55.00
Row 2
1. $195.00
2. $135.00
3. $22.00
4. $90.00
5. $125.00
Row 3
1. $45.00
2,4. $475.00
3. $775.00
5. $70.00
Row 4
1. $55.00
2. $210.00
3. $55.00
4. $40.00
5. $70.00
PLATE 31
Row 1
1. $85.00
2. $55.00
3. $125.00
Row 2
1. $190.00
2. $65.00
3. $330.00
4. $70.00
5. $80.00
6. $65.00
Row 3
1. $340.00
2. $220.00
3. $140.00
4. $1,850.00
5. $35.00
6. $210.00
Row 4
1,3. $220.00
2. $200.00
PLATE 32
Row 1
1. $200.00
2. $180.00

3. $120.00
Row 2
1. $1,275.00
2-6. $320.00
7. $100.00
Row 3
1,3. $210.00
2. $235.00
Row 4
1. $80.00
2. $80.00
3. $200.00
4. $75.00
5. $185.00
6. $1,175.00
PLATE 33
Row 1
1. $350.00
2. $300.00
3. $40.00
4. $120.00
5. $65.00
Row 2
1. $75.00
2. $75.00
3. $45.00
4. $1,425.00
5. $45.00
6. $55.00
Row 3
1. $30.00
2. $45.00
3. $45.00
4. $40.00
5. $85.00
6. $48.00
7. $115.00
8. $60.00
9. $45.00
10. $40.00
Row 4
1. $48.00
2. $160.00
3. $25.00
4. $250.00
5. $120.00
6. $48.00
7. $45.00
PLATE 34
Row 1
1. $75.00
2. $85.00
3. $100.00
4. $90.00
5. $50.00
Row 2
1. $55.00
2. $50.00
3. $60.00
4. $45.00
5. $135.00
6. $55.00
7. $55.00
8. $65.00
Row 3
1. $1,050.00
Row 4
1. $130.00
2. $35.00
3. $65.00
4. $75.00
5. $220.00
6. $65.00
7. $50.00
8. $95.00
PLATE 35
Row 1
1. $700.00
2. $160.00

3. $550.00
Row 2
1. $230.00
2,4. $350.00
3. $185.00
5. $175.00
Row 3
1. $320.00
2. $4,000.00
3. $950.00
PLATE 36
Row 1
1-3. $700.00
4. $90.00
5. $85.00
6. $720.00
Row 2
1. $190.00
2. $700.00
3. $175.00
Row 3
1. $375.00
2. $110.00
3. $315.00
Row 4
1. $420.00
2. $55.00
3. $180.00
4. $65.00
5. $525.00
PLATE 37
Row 1
1,3. $250.00
2. $375.00
Row 2
1. $375.00
2. $90.00
3. $220.00
Row 3
1. $180.00
2. $420.00
3. $50.00
PLATE 38
Row 1
1. $625.00
2. $45.00
3. $275.00
4. $135.00
5. $650.00
Row 2
1. $52.00
2. $85.00
3. $275.00
4. $80.00
5. $275.00
Row 3
1. $45.00
2. $130.00
3. $110.00
4. $395.00
5. $85.00
6. $45.00
7. $90.00
8. $110.00
Row 4
1,5. $160.00
2. $32.00
3. $300.00
4. $45.00
PLATE 39
Row 1
1. $130.00
2. $230.00
3. $135.00
Row 2
1. $95.00
2,4. $550.00
3. $165.00

5. $85.00
Row 3
1,4 $275.00
2. $220.00
3. $375.00
Row 4
1. $75.00
2. $75.00
3-7. $300.00
8. $200.00

PLATE 40
Row 1
1. $45.00
2,4. $80.00
3. $85.00
5. $40.00
Row 2
1. $30.00
2. $45.00
3. $110.00
4. $240.00
Row 3
1. $40.00
2. $45.00
3. $15.00
4. $40.00
5. $20.00
6. $30.00
7. $45.00

PLATE 41
Row 1
1. $20.00
2. $60.00
3. $50.00
4. $32.00
Row 2
1. $33.00
2. $25.00
3. $44.00
4. $35.00
5. $60.00
6. $420.00
7. $25.00
8. $42.00
Row 3
1. $40.00
2. $35.00
3. $20.00
4. $20.00
5. $45.00
6. $20.00
7. $35.00
8. $45.00

PLATE 42
Row 1
1. $20.00
2. $45.00
3. $20.00
4. $245.00
5. $50.00
6. $33.00
7. $22.00
Row 2
1. $60.00
2. $35.00
3. $35.00
4. $25.00
5. $40.00
Row 3
1. $42.00
2. $35.00
3. $38.00
4. $33.00
5. $43.00
6. $37.00

PLATE 43
Row 1
1,3. $130.00

---

2. $95.00
Row 2
1. $65.00
2. $50.00
3. $340.00
4. $85.00
5. $63.00
Row 3
1. $23.00
2. $24.00
3. $45.00
4. $38.00
5. $20.00

PLATE 44
Row 1
1. $75.00
2. $54.00
3. $68.00
4. $35.00
Row 2
1. $72.00
2. $350.00
3. $60.00
4. $26.00
5. $90.00
Row 3
1. $70.00
2,4. $550.00
3. $780.00
5. $52.00
Row4
1. $20.00
2,4. $80.00
3. $55.00
5. $50.00

PLATE 45
Row 1
1. $125.00
2. $220.00
3. $52.00
Row 2
1. $80.00
2. $60.00
3. $165.00
Row 3
1. $75.00
2. $120.00
3. $85.00
4. $75.00
Row 4
1. $70.00
2. $50.00
3. $120.00
4. $85.00
5. $38.00
6. $40.00
7. $40.00

PLATE 46
Row 1
1. $48.00
2. $58.00
3. $35.00
Row 2
1. $33.00
2. $48.00
3,5. $50.00
4. $65.00
6. $43.00
7. $28.00
Row 3
1,5. $70.00
2,4. $80.00
3. $55.00
Row 4
1. $65.00
2. $27.00
3. $34.00
4. $50.00

---

5. $25.00
6. $38.00
7. $75.00

PLATE 47
Row 1
1. $30.00
2. $30.00
3. $25.00
4,6. $70.00
5. $40.00
Row 2
1. $75.00
2. $75.00
3. $115.00
4. $100.00
5. $275.00
6. $375.00
7. $105.00
Row 3
1. $36.00
2. $95.00
3. $75.00
4. $37.00
5. $27.00
Row 4
1. $48.00
2. $54.00
3. $58.00

PLATE 48
Row 1
1. $85.00
2. $80.00
3. $80.00
4. $80.00
Row 2
1. $340.00
2. $130.00
3. $400.00
4. $230.00
5. $365.00
Row 3
1. $150.00
2. $1,200.00
3. $385.00

PLATE 49
Row 1
1. $200.00
2. $110.00
3. $270.00
4. $150.00
5. $260.00
Row 2
1. $165.00
2. $190.00
3. $210.00
4. $140.00
5. $175.00
Row 3
1. $45.00
2. $95.00
3. $80.00
4. $80.00
5. $85.00
6. $85.00
Row 4
1. $60.00
2. $52.00
3. $48.00
4. $60.00
5. $475.00
6. $48.00

PLATE 50
No prices due to lack of trading

PLATE 51
Row 1
1. $65.00
2. $50.00

---

3. $40.00
4. $40.00
5. $65.00
6. $44.00
Row 2
1. $55.00
2. $40.00
3. $40.00
4. $875.00
5. $85.00
6. $75.00
Row 3
1. $60.00
2. $130.00
3. $40.00
4. $45.00
5. $195.00
6. $200.00
Row 4
1. $50.00
2. $65.00
3. $50.00
4. $150.00
5. $90.00
6. $120.00

PLATE 52
Row 1
1. $26.00
2. $25.00
3. $250.00
4. $50.00
Row 2
1. $110.00
2. $25.00
3. $25.00
4. $30.00
Row 3
1. $130.00
2. $65.00
3. $60.00
Row 4
1. $80.00
2. $40.00
3. $70.00
4. $45.00
5. $75.00
6. $55.00

PLATE 53
Row 1
1. $120.00
2. $42.00
3. $85.00
4. $65.00
5. $60.00
Row 2
1. $650.00
2. $65.00
3. $40.00
4. $55.00
Row 3
1,2. $185.00
3. $80.00
4. $150.00

PLATE 54
Row 1
1. $175.00
2. $230.00
3. $525.00
4. $110.00
5. $425.00
Row 2
1. $400.00
2. $350.00
3. $50.00
4. $40.00
5. $150.00
Row 3
1. $180.00

---

2. $125.00
3. $25.00
4. $45.00
5. $22.00
Row 4
1. $25.00
2. $45.00
3. $120.00
4. $345.00

PLATE 55
Row 1
1. $55.00
2. $80.00
3. $25.00
4. $50.00
5. $85.00
6. $23.00
Row 2
1. $130.00
2. $130.00
3. $30.00
Row 3
1. $90.00
2. $40.00
3. $23.00
4. $23.00
5. $33.00
6. $54.00
Row 4
1. $330.00
2. $105.00
3. $60.00
4. $35.00
5. $45.00
6. $270.00

PLATE 56
Row 1
1. $25.00
2. $28.00
3. $30.00
4. $25.00
5. $25.00
6. $25.00
7. $35.00
8. $25.00
9. $24.00
10. $25.00
11. $17.00
12. $17.00
Row 2
1. $40.00
2. $40.00
3. $40.00
4. $40.00
5. $40.00
6. $30.00
7. $31.00
8. $29.00
9. $28.00
10. $33.00
11. $31.00
12. $35.00
Row 3
1-4. $54.00
5. $30.00
6. $25.00
7. $30.00
8. $30.00
9. $32.00
10. $22.00
11. $22.00
12. $25.00
Row 4
1. $15.00
2. $17.00
3. $15.00
4. $15.00
5. $15.00
6. $15.00

7-10. $50.00

PLATE 57
Row 1
1. $340.00
2. $75.00
3. $345.00
4. $320.00
5. $350.00
6. $200.00
7. $275.00
Row 2
1. $800.00
2,4. $850.00
3. $480.00
5. $220.00
Row 3
1. $185.00
2. $100.00
3. $425.00
4. $420.00
5. $165.00
6. $575.00
7. $550.00
Row 4
1. $350.00
2. $175.00
3. $250.00
4. $230.00
5. $140.00
6. $575.00
7. $185.00
8. $250.00

PLATE 58
Row 1
1. $380.00
2. $18.00
3. $25.00
4. $55.00
5. $22.00
6. $54.00
7. $25.00
Row 2
1. $550.00
2. $850.00
3. $185.00
4. $185.00
5. $220.00
Row 3
1. $345.00
2. $200.00
3. $820.00
4. $625.00
5. $190.00
6. $225.00
Row 4
1. $650.00
2. $950.00
3. $440.00
4. $265.00
5. $650.00

PLATE 59
Row 1
1. $40.00
2. $65.00
3. $40.00
4. $45.00
5. $55.00
6. $42.00
7. $40.00
Row 2
1. $140.00
2. $45.00
3. $75.00
4. $35.00
5. $105.00
6. $65.00
7. $105.00
Row 3
1. $48.00

---

2. $40.00
3. $40.00
4. $100.00
5. $90.00
6. $40.00
7. $40.00
8. $30.00
9. $56.00
10. $15.00
Row 4
1. $25.00
2. $75.00
3. $180.00
4. $12.00
5. $35.00
6. $58.00
7. $35.00
8. $145.00
9. $40.00
10. $22.00
Row 5
1. $42.00
2. $42.00
3. $36.00
4. $36.00
5. $58.00
6. $72.00
7. $52.00
8. $50.00
9. $62.00
10. $37.00
11. $40.00
12. $35.00
13. $57.00
14. $52.00
15. $75.00
16. $73.00
Row 6
1. $22.00
2. $24.00
3. $28.00
4. $23.00
5. $22.00
6. $135.00
7. $95.00
8. $95.00
9. $85.00
10. $82.00
Row 7
1. $45.00
2. $25.00
3. $40.00
4. $25.00
5. $20.00
6. $56.00
7. $40.00

PLATE 60
Row 1
1. $950.00
2. $900.00
Row 2
1. $130.00
2. $140.00
3. $135.00
Row 3
1. $575.00
2. $480.00
3. $1,250.00
Row 4
1. $450.00
2. $50.00
3. $50.00
4. $155.00
5. $120.00